Java™ and XML Data Binding

Related titles from O'Reilly

Ant: The Definitive Guide

Building Java™ Enterprise Applications

Database Programming with JDBC™ and Java™

Developing Java Beans™

Enterprise JavaBeans™

J2ME™ in a Nutshell

Java™ 2D Graphics

Java™ & SOAP

Java™ & XML

Java™ and XSLT

Java™ Cookbook

Java™ Cryptography

Java™ Distributed Computing

Java™ Enterprise in a Nutshell

Java™ Examples in a Nutshell

Java™ Foundation Classes in a Nutshell

Java™ I/O

Java™ in a Nutshell

Java™ Internationalization

Java™ Message Service

Java™ Network Programming

Java™ Performance Tuning

Java™ Programming with Oracle SQLJ

Java™ RMI

Java™ Security

JavaServer™ Pages

JavaServer™ Pages Pocket Reference

Java™ Servlet Programming

Java™ Swing

Java™ Threads

Learning Java™

Also available

The Java™ Enterprise CD Bookshelf

Java™ and XML Data Binding

Brett McLaughlin

Beijing · Cambridge · Farnham · Köln · Paris · Sebastopol · Taipei · Tokyo

Java™ and XML Data Binding
by Brett McLaughlin

Published by O'Reilly & Associates, Inc., 1005 Gravenstein Highway North, Sebastopol, CA 95472.

O'Reilly & Associates books may be purchased for educational, business, or sales promotional use. Online editions are also available for most titles (*safari.oreilly.com*). For more information contact our corporate/institutional sales department: (800) 998-9938 or *corporate@oreilly.com*.

Editor:	Mike Loukides
Production Editor:	Ann Schirmer
Cover Designer:	Hanna Dyer
Interior Designer:	Melanie Wang

Printing History:

May 2002:	First Edition.

ISBN: 0-596-00278-5

[M]

Table of Contents

Preface

XML data binding. Yes, it's yet another Java and XML API. Haven't we seen enough of this by now? If you don't like SAX or DOM, you can use JDOM or dom4j. If they don't suit you, SOAP and WSDL provide some neat features. But then there is JAXP, JAXR, and XML-RPC. If you just can't get the swing of those, perhaps RSS, portlets, Cocoon, Barracuda, XMLC, or JSP with XML-based tag libraries is the way to go.

The point of that ridiculous opening is that you, as a developer, should expect some justification for buying yet another XML book, on yet another XML API. The market seems flooded with books like this, and the torrent has yet to slow down. And while I realize that I use circular reasoning when insisting that this API is important (I did write this book on it), that's just what I'm going to do.

XML data binding has taken the XML world by storm. Thousands of programmers simply threw up their hands trying to track SAX, DOM, JDOM, dom4J, JAXP, and the rest. It's become increasingly difficult to parse a silly little XML document, rather than increasingly simple. If it's not namespaces that get you, it's whitespace. Is that carriage return after my element name significant? Well, it depends on whether you specify a DTD; oh, you used an XML Schema? Well, we don't support that yet. I'm sure you know exactly what I'm talking about.

The reason why XML data binding is important, and so remarkably different from other approaches, is because it gets you from XML to business data with no stops in between. You don't have to deal with angle brackets, entity references, or namespaces. A data binding framework converts from XML to data, without your messing around under the hood. For most developers who try to get into XML without spending months doing it, data binding is just the answer you are looking for.

This book covers data binding from front to back, giving you the ins and outs of what may turn out to be the API that makes XML accessible to even the newest programmers. You'll learn how to perform basic conversions from Java to XML, all the way to using various frameworks for advanced transformations and mappings. It's all in this (nicely compact) book, without lots of wasted words and frilly examples. If you want to use data binding, this book is for you. If you don't, well, put it down and go pick up about ten other books so you can manipulate XML some other way. I think the choice is obvious; so get started!

Organization

I begin this book with a brief explanation of what data binding is and what other APIs are in the XML field. From there, I provide an extensive look at Sun's JAXB, that company's data binding framework. You'll learn every option and every switch to use this package. Then, to round out your data binding skills, I examine three other popular open source data binding frameworks, each with its strengths and weaknesses.

Chapter 1, *Introduction*

> This chapter is a basic introduction to XML data binding and to the general Java and XML landscape that currently exists. It details the basic Java and XML APIs available and organizes them by the general usage situations to which they are applied. It also details setting up for the rest of the book.

Chapter 2, *Theory and Concepts*

> This chapter is the (only) theoretical chapter in the book. It details the difference between data-driven and business-driven APIs and explains when one model is preferable over the other. It then explains how constraint modeling fits into the data binding picture and how data binding makes XML invisible to the application developer.

Chapter 3, *Generating Classes*

> This chapter is the first detailed introduction to data binding. It explains the process of taking a set of XML constraints and converting those constraints into a set of Java source files. It details how this is accomplished using the JAXB API and then explains how the resultant source files can be compiled and used in a Java application.

Chapter 4, *Unmarshalling*

> This chapter continues the nuts-and-bolts approach to teaching data binding. It covers the process of converting XML documents to Java objects and how the data should be modeled for correct conversion. It also details the use of resultant Java objects.

Chapter 5, *Marshalling*

> This chapter details the conversion from Java objects to XML documents. It explains the overall process flow, as well as the implementation-level steps involved in marshalling. It also covers creating data binding process loops, ensuring that data binding can occur repeatedly in applications.

Chapter 6, *Binding Schemas*

This chapter focuses on binding schemas and how they can customize transformation from XML to Java. Every option in binding schemas is examined and discussed both technically and practically.

Chapter 7, *Zeus*

This chapter begins an exploration of alternate data binding packages with Zeus. The coverage is based on the explored JAXB concepts and compares Zeus operation to the techniques already discussed in previous chapters. Particular attention is paid to Zeus enhancements that are not in the JAXB API.

Chapter 8, *Castor*

This chapter continues exploration of alternate data binding implementations by looking at Castor. This open source alternative was the first major data binding implementation available and offers many features not present in JAXB. These features, as well as process variations, are all covered in this chapter.

Chapter 9, *Quick*

Quick is another open source data binding API, and this chapter details its ins and outs. You'll see that Quick offers ideas and processes that are entirely different from most data binding frameworks and you'll learn how those differences can be put to work in your applications.

Chapter 10, *Looking Forward*

This chapter looks at the future of data binding. It covers the final version of JAXB, as well as expectations for the next JAXB release. It also covers how alternate data binding implementations are likely to change with a JAXB 1.0 release and looks at JAXB in light of the J2EE platform.

Appendix A, *Tools Reference*

This appendix details all the options for the tools provided by various data binding APIs. It can be used as a quick reference for each chapter and for your own programming projects.

Appendix B, *Quick Source Files*

This appendix details several source files used by the examples in the Quick chapter.

Conventions Used in This Book

I use the following font conventions in this book:

Italic is used for:

- Unix pathnames, filenames, and program names
- Internet addresses, such as domain names and URLs
- New terms where they are defined

Boldface is used for:

- Emphasis in source code (including XML).

`Constant width` is used for:

- Command lines and options that should be typed verbatim
- Names and keywords in Java programs, including method names, variable names, and class names
- XML element names and tags, attribute names, and other XML constructs that appear as they would within an XML document

 This symbol indicates a tip.

 This symbol indicates a warning.

Comments and Questions

Please address comments and questions concerning this book to the publisher:

O'Reilly & Associates, Inc.
1005 Gravenstein Highway North
Sebastopol, CA 95472
(800) 998-9938 (in the United States or Canada)
(707) 829-0515 (international/local)
(707) 829-0104 (fax)

There is a web page for this book, which lists errata, examples, or any additional information. You can access this page at:

http://www.oreilly.com/catalog/javaxmldatabind

To comment or ask technical questions about this book, send email to:

bookquestions@oreilly.com

For more information about books, conferences, Resource Centers, and the O'Reilly Network, see the O'Reilly web site at:

http://www.oreilly.com

Acknowledgments

At some point, you start writing acknowledgments and taking them for granted. Then, you realize that this is the only section that most of your family will read and understand, and you slow down and get them right.

First, for the technical folks. Mike Loukides and Kyle Hart manage to get me to write these books, and write them fast, without exploding. Thanks guys, but I'm going on vacation now! I had two incredible reviewers on this book, and they really transformed it from OK to great, in my opinion. Thanks to Michael Daudel and Niel Bornstein for persevering under major time constraints and still generating really good comments.

My family is always amazing, and always interested, even though I know they wonder what it is I write about. My parents, Larry and Judy McLaughlin, taught me to read and write and to do them both well. I'm eternally indebted, as are my readers! My aunt, Sarah Jane Burden, is always there to state the obvious in a way that makes me laugh, and my sister has simply grown up as I have written these books. She's now teaching math, probably producing more programmers and writers. I'm proud of you, Sis!

The other side of my family has been there for me since I met them, especially since we live in the same town. Gary and Shirley Greathouse, my father- and mother-in-law, keep me laughing as well, mostly at the strange things they manage to make their computers do ("So, there's this black screen with little rectangles—what do I do now?"). Quinn, Joni, Laura, and Lonnie are all fun to be around, and that's saying a lot. And little Nate, my first-ever nephew, is absolutely the coolest little guy on the planet, at least for a few more months.

My wife, Leigh, has lived with a husband who has written for more hours a day than he spends with her, for nearly three years, and has always loved and supported me. That's saying a lot, because I'm a royal pain most of the time. I love you, honey. And as for that "few more months" comment, I've got a little boy coming in June (2002) who should make life even more exciting. When you read this one day, kiddo, remember that I love you.

Last and most important, to the Lord who got me this far: even so, come, Lord Jesus. I'm ready to go home.

CHAPTER 1

Introduction

With the wealth of interest in XML in the last few years, developers have begun to crave more than the introductory books on XML and Java that are currently available. While a chapter or two on SAX, some basic information on JAXP, and a section on web services was sufficient when these APIs were developed, programmers now want more. Specifically, there is a huge amount of interest in XML data binding, a new set of APIs that allows XML to be dealt with in Java simply and intuitively, without worrying about brackets and syntactical issues. The result is a need in the developer community for an extensive, technically focused documentation set on using data binding; examples are no longer just helpful, but a critical, required part of this documentation set. This book will provide that technical documentation, ready for immediate use in your application programming.

To fill this need, I want to start off on the right foot and dive into some technical material. This chapter will give you basic information about existing XML APIs and how they relate to XML data binding. From there, I move on to the four basic facets of data binding, which the first half of this book focuses on. Finally, to get you ready for the extensive examples I walk you through, I devote the last portion of this chapter to the APIs, projects, and tools you'll need throughout the rest of the book. From there on, I assault you with examples and technical details, so I hope you're ready.

Low-Level APIs

By the simple fact that you've picked up this book, I assume that you are interested in working with XML from within your Java programs and applications. However, it's probably not too smart to assume that you're a Java and XML expert (yet—although picking up my *Java and XML* book could help!), so I want to take you through the application programming interfaces (APIs) available for working with XML from Java. I'll start by detailing what I will henceforth refer to as *low-level APIs*. These APIs allow you direct access to an XML document's *data*, as well as its *structure*.

To illustrate this concept a little more clearly, consider the following simple XML document:

```xml
<?xml version="1.0"?>

<songs>
  <song>
    <title>The Finishing Touch</title>
    <artist type="Band">Sound Doctrine</artist>
  </song>

  <song>
    <title>Change Your World</title>
    <artist type="Solo">Eric Clapton</artist>
    <artist type="Solo">Babyface</artist>
  </song>

  <song>
    <title>The Chasing Song</title>
    <artist type="Band">Andy Peterson</artist>
  </song>
</songs>
```

An Abridged Dictionary

Before going further, you should know a couple of terms. For those of you familiar with XML, this should be old hat, but for XML newbies, this should prevent future confusion.

Well formed
> An XML document that follows all the rules of XML syntax, such as closing every open element in the correct order.

Valid
> An XML document that follows the constraints set out for it by a DTD or XML Schema. If the document does not follow these constraints, it is *invalid*.

Anything else that confuses you can be found in a quick page, either through O'Reilly's *Learning XML*, by Erik Ray, or *XML in a Nutshell*, by Elliotte Rusty Harold and W. Scott Means. I recommend having one or both nearby as you go through this book.

Using a low-level API, you could access the textual content of the second artist element in the second song. That's the data of the document. In addition, a low-level API lets you change the name of the third song element to folkSong, or move the second song element before the first one. In other words, you have direct access, though methods like setName() and getChild(), to the document itself. These actions don't involve the data in the document, but the structure. Understanding this concept is important because you'll see in a moment that a whole set of APIs don't allow this access and are aimed at a very different set of use cases.

In general, using a low-level API is a little more complex than using high-level APIs (discussed in a moment), as it requires more XML knowledge. Since you have access to a document's structure, it's not too hard to create an invalid document. Additionally, you are going to spend as much, if not more, time dealing with document structure and rules of XML than with the actual data. This means that in a typical application, you're spending more time thinking about structure than solving any given business problem. For these reasons, low-level APIs are usually most common in infrastructure tasks or when setting up communication in messaging. When it comes to solving a specific business problem, higher-level APIs (see the next section) are often more appropriate. With that in mind, let me give you the rundown on the major low-level APIs that are currently available.

Streamed Data

The grandfather of all Java-based low-level APIs is the Simple API for XML (SAX). SAX was the first major API released that has any sort of following, and it remains the basic building block of pretty much all other APIs. SAX is based on a streaming input and reads information from an XML input source piece by piece. In other words, information is sent to the SAX interfaces as the related input stream (or reader) gets it. To use SAX for parsing, you register various *handler implementations* for handling content, errors, entities, and so forth. Each interface is made up of several callback methods, which receive information about specific data being sent to the parser, such as character data, the start of an element and the end of a prefix mapping. Your SAX-based application can then use that information to perform business tasks within the callback method implementations.

The advantage to this stream-based approach is raw, blazing speed. SAX easily outstrips any other API in performance (and don't let anyone tell you differently). Because it reads a document piece by piece, making that data available as soon as it is encountered, your applications don't have to wait for the complete document to be parsed to operate upon the data. However, that speed carries a price: complexity. SAX is probably the hardest API for developers to wrap their heads around, and even then, many have trouble writing efficient SAX code. Because data is read in a streaming fashion, your callback methods won't have access to an element's children, its parent, or its siblings. Instead, you have to build up some in-memory stack if you want to keep an idea of tree location. Because of this complexity, it's easy to ignore important data or make mistakes when reading in data. As a result of this complexity, many developers pass up SAX and prefer an API that provides an in-memory model of an XML document. You can learn more about SAX online at *http://www.saxproject.org*.

Modeled Data

Java and XML APIs that model XML data are generally more popular, as their learning curve is much smaller. The oldest and most popular of these is the Document

Object Model (DOM). This API was developed by the World Wide Web Consortium and provides a complete in-memory model of an XML document. DOM is *not* a parser (and neither is SAX); it requires an XML parser that supplies a *DOM implementation* to operate. When the parser completes its reading of an XML document, the result is a DOM tree. This tree models an XML document, with parent elements having children, textual nodes, comments, and other XML constructs. You can easily walk up and down a DOM tree using the DOM API and generally move around easily. Because you have to wait on a complete parse before using a DOM, it is often slower than using SAX; because it creates objects for each XML structure, it takes a lot more memory to operate. However, these disadvantages are paired with a significantly easier programming model, a means to traverse the content of the DOM tree, and several implementations that offer various options. For example, Apache Xerces offers a "deferred DOM," which makes some trade-offs to reduce the memory overhead when using DOM. For more on DOM, check out *http://www.w3.org/DOM*.

Recently, developers have moved away from DOM. This is because DOM has some quirks that are not familiar to Java developers; this isn't surprising, considering that DOM is specifically built to work across multiple languages (Java, C, and Java-Script). As a result, some of the choices made, such as the lack of support for Java Collections, don't sit well with Java developers. The result has been two APIs that both are object models aimed squarely at Java and XML developers. The first, JDOM (*http://www.jdom.org*), is focused on simplicity and avoiding interfaces in programming. The second, dom4j (*http://www.dom4j.org*), keeps the DOM-style interfaces, but (like JDOM) incorporates Java collections and other Java-style features. I prefer JDOM, but then I cofounded it, so I'm a bit biased! In any case, DOM, JDOM, and dom4j all offer more user-friendly approaches to XML than does SAX, at the expense of memory and performance.

Abstracted Data

Completing the run through low-level APIs, the third model is what I refer to as *abstracted data*. This type of API is represented by Sun's Java API for XML Parsing (JAXP). It doesn't offer new functionality over the streamed data (SAX) or modeled data (DOM and company), but abstracts these APIs and makes them vendor-neutral. Because SAX and DOM are based on Java interfaces, different vendors provide implementations of them. These implementations often result in code that relies on a specific vendor parsing class, which ruins any chance of code portability. JAXP offers abstractions of the DOM and SAX APIs, allowing you to easily change parser vendors and API implementations.

The latest version of JAXP, 1.1, offers this same abstracted data model over XML transformations, but that's a little beyond the scope of this book. In terms of pros and cons in using JAXP, I'd recommend it if you will work with SAX or DOM and can get the latest version of JAXP. It helps you avoid the hard-coded sort of problems that can creep in when working directly with a vendor's implementation classes. In any case, this brief little whirlwind tour should give you at least a basic understanding of the available low-level Java and XML APIs. With these APIs in mind, let me move up the rung a bit to high-level APIs.

High-Level APIs

So far, the APIs I've discussed have been driven by the data in an XML document. They give you flexibility and power, but also generally require that you write more code to access that power. However, XML has been around long enough that some pretty common use cases have begun to crop up. For example, configuration files are one of the most common uses of XML around. Here's an example:

```xml
<?xml version="1.0"?>

<ejb-jar>
  <entity>
    <description>This is the Account EJB which represents
    the information which is kept for each Customer</description>

    <display-name>TheAccount</display-name>
    <ejb-name>TheAccount</ejb-name>
    <home>com.sun.j2ee.blueprints.customer.account.ejb.AccountHome</home>
    <remote>com.sun.j2ee.blueprints.customer.account.ejb.Account</remote>
    <ejb-class>com.sun.j2ee.blueprints.customer.account.ejb.AccountEJB</ejb-class>
    <persistence-type>Bean</persistence-type>
    <prim-key-class>java.lang.String</prim-key-class>
    <reentrant>False</reentrant>
    <env-entry>
      <env-entry-name>ejb/account/AccountDAOClass</env-entry-name>
      <env-entry-type>java.lang.String</env-entry-type>
      <env-entry-value>
        com.sun.j2ee.blueprints.customer.account.dao.AccountDAOImpl
      </env-entry-value>
    </env-entry>

    <resource-ref>
      <res-ref-name>jdbc/EstoreDataSource</res-ref-name>
      <res-type>javax.sql.DataSource</res-type>
      <res-auth>Container</res-auth>
    </resource-ref>
  </entity>
</ejb-jar>
```

In this case, the example is a deployment descriptor from Sun's PetStore J2EE example application. Here, there isn't any data processing that needs to occur; an application that deploys this application wants to know the description, the display name, the home interface, and the remote interface. However, you can see that these are simply the names of the various elements.

Instead of spending time parsing and traversing, it would be much easier to code something like this:

```
List entities = ejbJar.getEntityList( );
for (Iterator i = entities.iterator( ); i.hasNext( ); ) {
    Entity entity = (Entity)i.next( );
    String displayName = entity.getDisplayName( );
    String homeInterface = entity.getHome( );
    // etc.
}
```

Instead of working with XML, the Java classes use the business purpose of the document rather than the data. This approach is obviously easier and has become quite popular. Remember, though, that the high-level approach works only in the situation shown here. If you have to perform more complex processing, are filtering data, or have to perform one of a thousand other less-than-routine tasks, these higher-level APIs become less useful. As a result, you'll want to pair the APIs mentioned in this section with the lower-level APIs from the last, thus forming a complete set of tools.

Mapped Data

The most common high-level API, and the one that seems to be gaining the most momentum, is mapping data from an XML document to Java classes. This is the case I just showed you: an XML document is represented by business-driven Java classes, and the data is mapped from the document into the member variables of these Java classes. This mapping of data is generally known as *data binding*. When working from an XML data store, it is referred to as *XML data binding*.* I won't spend too much time on this topic here, as you've got the rest of the book to get the nitty-gritty on mapping-based solutions.

You should realize that under the hood of these low-level APIs, SAX (and sometimes DOM, JDOM, or dom4j) is used to parse XML data. You still have to have parsing and processing; however, data binding hides these details and delivers data to you in a nice, business-driven package. To fully utilize these sorts of APIs, you'll probably need to at least know basic SAX concepts like entity resolution and validation. As with any other API, the more you know about what occurs beneath the public interface, the better you can use the API and the more performance you can squeeze out.

Messaged Data

I don't want to open too big a can of worms by getting into web services, but you should know about an entirely different type of higher-level API. In a message-based API, XML is used as the interchange medium for data. For example, a Java array that

---

* Although they won't get much attention in this book, there are also binding packages for converting JDBC rowsets to Java, SQL results to Java, or LDAP queries to Java—just about anything you can imagine. Future books from O'Reilly will cover many of these emerging technologies.

needs to be sent to another application might normally use RMI or something similar. However, if network traffic is prohibited except via HTTP (usually on port 80), or if the data must be sent to a non-Java application, XML can provide a data format for exchanging the contents of that array. For example, here's an XML representation of an array with four elements, all of various types:

```
<array>
  <data>
    <value><i4>12</i4></value>
    <value><string>Egypt</string></value>
    <value><boolean>0</boolean></value>
    <value><i4>-31</i4></value>
  </data>
</array>
```

This data can then be sent as a message, and any application component that is set up to receive XML messages can use this data. If this sort of communication interests you, check out the Simple Object Access Protocol (SOAP) (*http://www.w3.org/2000/xp*), and XML-RPC (*http://www.xml-rpc.com*). Both offer XML-based messaging and allow you to interact with XML data at a higher level than SAX or object-based APIs.

If you want to find out more about web services, you can pick up O'Reilly's *Java and Web Services*, by Tyler Jewell and David Chappell, or *Programming Web Services with XML-RPC*, by Simon St.Laurent, Joe Johnston, and Edd Dumbill. Additionally, a variety of resources on the Web deal with these technologies. You'll also want to check out Universal Description, Discovery, and Integration (UDDI) registries and the Web Service Description Language (WSDL). I mention these to point out how many XML formats there are; for every format, you'll need an API to access and manipulate the data within differing documents. You'll want to be able to use both low- and high-level APIs to accomplish this. Now that I've run through the basic APIs, let me get to the business of talking about XML data binding.

What Is Data Binding?

Before starting with the meat of the book, let me give you a basic introduction to data binding and the four concepts that make up a data binding package:

- Source file/class generation
- Unmarshalling
- Marshalling
- Binding schemas

I'll focus on each of these over the next several chapters, but I wanted to give you a bit of a preview here. You'll want to get an idea of the big picture so you can see how these components fit together.

Class Generation

I've already mentioned that the basic idea of data binding is to take an XML document and convert it to an instance of a Java object. Furthermore, that Java class is tailored to a business need and generally matches up with the element and attribute naming in the related XML document. Of course, I conveniently skipped over where that class comes from; this is where class generation comes in. In the most common XML data binding scenario, this class is not hand coded (that's quite a pain, right?). Instead, a data binding tool that will generate this source file (or source files) for you is provided.

In a nutshell, data binding packages allow you to take a set of XML constraints (DTD, XML Schema, etc.) and create a set of Java source files from these constraints. I'll dive deeper into the specifics of this subject in Chapter 3. In general, it works like this: an element is defined in a DTD called dealer-name, and a Java class called DealerName is generated. An XML Schema defines the servlet element as having an attribute called id and a child element named description, and the resultant Java class (Servlet) has a getId() method as well as a getDescription() method. You get the idea—a mapping is made between the structure laid out by the XML constraint document and a set of Java classes. You can then compile these classes and begin converting between XML and Java.

Unmarshalling

Once you've got your generated classes compiled and on your Java Virtual Machine's (JVM's) classpath, you're ready to convert XML documents to Java classes. This process is called *unmarshalling* in the data binding world.* The process is based on starting with an XML document. This document should conform to the XML constraints used to generate Java classes, referred to in the class generation section. If it doesn't meet these constraints, you're going to get errors as elements, attributes, and character data in the XML document won't match up with the structure of the generated Java classes. Most data binding packages offer an option to validate an XML document before unmarshalling it to ensure you don't run into this problem. I'll focus on this and the other details of unmarshalling in Chapter 4.

Lest you think that all of your existing business objects are wasted, it is possible to unmarshal an XML document into an existing Java class (or classes). This is a common scenario when you already have a Java-based application and want to persist some of your objects to XML (like Enterprise JavaBeans or other data-related

---

* If you forget which way is marshalling and which is unmarshalling, remember that it's *XML* data binding. Everything starts and ends with XML, so converting to XML is the "normal" direction, resulting in simple marshalling. Converting from XML is the reverse direction, so you are *un*marshalling. For some reason, thinking of it this way keeps me straight.

objects). You can either structure your XML to match your existing Java object hierarchy or use a binding schema (covered later in this chapter). While not all data binding packages support this handy approach to data binding, I'll spend some time in the later chapters of the book exploring it.

Marshalling

The reverse of the unmarshalling process is *marshalling*, which converts a Java object into an XML document representation. There's nothing too revolutionary here that you probably haven't already guessed. As with unmarshalling, many frameworks offer a validation option on generated Java classes that allows you to validate the data within your Java classes before trying to write them out to XML. That ensures that the resultant XML documents still match up with the constraints used to generate Java classes in the first place. Some extra data carried around by these generated classes—such as the XML names of the related elements, DTD references, and namespace information—also tends to get marshalled to Java. This ensures that the Java classes marshal to XML documents that they are the same as (or as close as possible) the XML documents they came from.

Like unmarshalling, marshalling is a process that is often useful to classes that were not generated by a data binding framework. Like unmarshalling, only some frameworks support marshalling, but those that do can be incredibly useful. Generally, Java classes must follow some rules to be marshalled to XML, such as following the JavaBeans format (each data member has a getXXX() and setXXX() style method). However, if your classes conform to these rules, conversion to XML becomes simple. I'll focus on the nuts and bolts of marshalling in Chapter 5.

Binding Schemas

The final component of XML data binding is probably the most complex, but also the most powerful. A *binding schema* specifies details about how classes are generated from XML constraints. In the general case, an element named ejb-jar becomes an object named EjbJar. Some basic rules are applied to ensure legal Java names, but names are otherwise kept as true to the underlying XML as possible. Additionally, constraints such as those found in DTDs don't have type information applied (everything comes across as PCDATA, which is just character data). However, these basic rules are often not enough to create the Java business objects you want. In these cases, a binding schema can help.

A binding schema allows you to specify type conversions, name transformations, and specification of superclasses for generated objects. It allows the application of a richer set of rules, resulting in objects that more closely model your business needs. I'll spend all of Chapter 6 talking about this, so don't get too caught up in the details just yet. However, these binding schemas can allow you to convert XML to your already-coded Java classes, enforce type-checking even when a DTD doesn't, and a lot more. A binding schema takes data binding tools from trivial utility classes to full-blown persistence packages; all in all, they are the most powerful feature found in data binding packages.

How these schemas actually look and act depends largely (at least at this point in data binding evolution) upon the data binding implementation. Some binding schemas are actual XML Schema-style documents; others look like plain old XML documents. They are almost always represented by a physical XML-style document that is parsed in at the same time as the XML constraint model. It is then up to the data binding package to determine if the binding schema is packaged with generated classes or if the mappings are contained completely within generated source code. All of these details will be covered, for each binding package, in those packages' respective chapters.

What You'll Need

Finally, I want to let you know what packages, projects, and tools you'll need to work through this book. I'll address the installation and setup details of each in the chapters in which they are used, but you may want to go ahead and download these items before getting started (especially if you're on a slow Internet connection. That way, you're not stuck waiting on a download when you'd rather start a new chapter and example set.

Packages

First, you'll need Sun's JAXB. While JAXB is the least mature of the available data binding frameworks, Sun has often leveraged its Java influence to turn out what becomes the standard against which other packages are measured. Because of that, I'll spend the first half of this book discussing the various data binding components in light of their relation to JAXB. You can download the early-access version of JAXB at *http://java.sun.com/xml/jaxb/index.html*. The specification, as of this writing, is currently released as Version 0.21, and the implementation is a 1.0 release. I'll cover setting up JAXB for use with the examples in the next chapter.

Additionally, I'll cover three other data binding implementations, all open source projects. I do this for obvious reasons: I'm an open source advocate, it's easy for you to get, and as I've run into occasional bugs in writing this book, I've been able to fix them and save you some headaches. There are several commercial data binding applications, but I've yet to see anything that merits the high price tags they command (you will typically pay a low per-developer price, as well as a much higher one-time deployment fee). The open source packages have matured and serve me well in numerous production applications. You're welcome to use commercial packages, although the examples will have to be tweaked to work within those frameworks.

The first data binding implementation I'll cover is Enhydra Zeus in Chapter 7. I'm partial to this implementation, since I founded the project, but I will cover it and the other implementations as they relate to Sun's JAXB. You can download Zeus from *http://zeus.enhydra.org*; I'll use the latest CVS code for the examples in this book.

Following Zeus, I'll discuss Castor, a project from Exolab, in Chapter 8. Castor holds the notable honor of being the first major open source project in the data binding space and is fairly mature. Although Castor offers data binding from SQL and LDAP, I'll focus only on the XML portion of its data binding package. You can download Castor from *http://castor.exolab.org*; throughout the examples in Chapter 8, I'll use Version 0.9.3.9, which can be downloaded from the web site.

The final open source data binding package I'll cover is Quick, in Chapter 9. This package is a bit different from the others, as it defines a lot of semantics specific to Quick not found in JAXB, Zeus, or Castor. It also offers a solid environment for marshalling and unmarshalling objects without using class generation. You can download Quick from *http://jxquick.sourceforge.net/quick3*, and I'll use Version 4.3.0 for the examples in Chapter 9.

Tools

Finally, I recommend some tools for working through this book. While I've remained a stalwart proponent of using tools like vi, Emacs, and notepad for writing my XML and code, I've found IDEs more useful since I need to work with multiple files at the same time. Personally, I use jEdit (*http://www.jedit.org*), which has become my editor of choice. I'd also recommend you have some sort of XML editor around. I actually don't write my XML in these editors (they tend to be clumsy, in my opinion, but you may love them), but do use them for validation, checking well formedness, and other generic tasks. I've found jEdit and some of its plug-ins, as well as XMLSpy (*http://www.xmlspy.com*), helpful.

You'll also need a Java Development Kit for compiling and running the examples. You can download the UDK from *http://java.sun.com/j2se*; be sure to get the development kit, not just the runtime environment. I use JDK 1.3.1 for all of my examples, but not any features specific to the 1.3 version of the JDK (like dynamic proxies). I do, however, use code and frameworks that require Java 1.2 or greater for the included collection support. Any other productivity tools you use are up to you. Once you've got everything in place, turn the page and we'll get started.

CHAPTER 2

Theory and Concepts

In this chapter, I need to spend a little more time on some basic theory. I know you're ready to get to some code, but reading through this section will prepare you for the terms and concepts that I'll use later in the book and will also allow you to focus on application throughout the rest of the chapters. In the last chapter, you got a very quick rundown of both data-centric and business-centric APIs. In this chapter, I drill down into some of these APIs. However, instead of detailing what the APIs are, or how to use them, I focus on their relation to data binding. For example, most data binding packages allow you to set a SAX entity resolver, so I spend a little time detailing what that is. Since you won't ever need to use a SAX lexical handler, though, I skip right over that. Make sense?

In this chapter, I also explain how XML is modeled with constraints, cover the various constraint models currently available, and then funnel this into discussion of how constraints are critical to any data binding package. This will set the stage for Chapter 3, for which you need to have a good understanding of XML validation, DTDs, and XML Schema. Additionally, you'll learn about some of the newer constraint models that may affect data binding, like Relax NG.

Finally, I get a bit conceptual (but only briefly) and talk about the relevant factors for a good data binding API. You'll learn about runtime versus compile-time considerations, how versioning is a tricky issue in data binding, and what it takes to interoperate between data binding implementations. In addition to preparing you for a better understanding of the rest of the book, this section will be critical for those of you still deciding on a data binding implementation. Once you make it through this section, though, it's code the rest of the way through—I promise!

Foundational APIs

As I mentioned in the introductory chapter, data-centric XML APIs provide the lowest levels of interaction available to Java developers. Because of this, they form the backbone of many higher-level APIs, like data binding. Understanding them is important to effectively use a data binding tool. Not only does a keen understanding of these APIs help interpret error conditions and enhance performance, but it often allows you to set options on the unmarshalling and marshalling process that can drastically change the underlying parser's behavior. In this section, I cover the APIs that are fundamental to data binding and the concepts within these APIs that are critical to using a data binding framework.

SAX

SAX, the "old faithful" of Java and XML APIs, is critical to any good data binding package. It is most often used as the API that actually handles the process of unmarshalling an XML document into a Java object. Because SAX is a very fast, read-only API, it is perfect for providing a high-performance means of reading in XML data and setting member variables on generated Java classes. SAX is also lightweight in terms of packaging (while some parsers like Apache Xerces are large, the binary distribution of Crimson and other SAX-compliant parsers can manage to stay in the 200–400 KB range), which is great for running data binding in limited-memory environments (think mobile and embedded devices).

Because of this, you will often need to interact with SAX objects and methods, even at the data binding level. For example, SAX provides a means of setting an error handler, defined through the `org.xml.sax.ErrorHandler` interface. This allows parsing warnings and errors to be dealt with gracefully, rather than bringing a system to a grinding halt. Most data binding projects allow you to set an `ErrorHandler` implementation on a class to be unmarshalled (prior to the unmarshalling, of course) so you can customize error handling. In the Lutris Enhydra project, for example, the error handler implementation shown in Example 2-1 demonstrates how errors can be logged before being reported back to the application.

Example 2-1. The EnhydraErrorHandler class

```
package org.enhydra.util;

// Lutris Logging Package
import com.lutris.logging.LogChannel;
import com.lutris.logging.Logger;

// SAX imports
import org.xml.sax.ErrorHandler;
import org.xml.sax.SAXException;
import org.xml.sax.SAXParseException;

public class EnhydraErrorHandler implements ErrorHandler {

    private LogChannel logChannel;

    public EnhydraErrorHandler( ) {
        if (Logger.getCentralLogger( ) != null) {
```

Example 2-1. The EnhydraErrorHandler class (continued)

```
            logChannel = Logger.getCentralLogger( ).getChannel("Deployment");
        }
    }

    public void warning(SAXParseException e) throws SAXException {
        log(Logger.WARNING,
            new StringBuffer("Parsing Warning: ")
                .append(e.getMessage( ))
                .toString( ));
    }

    public void error(SAXParseException e) throws SAXException {
        log(Logger.WARNING,
            new StringBuffer("Parsing Error: ")
                .append(e.getMessage( ))
                .toString( ));
        throw e;
    }

    public void fatalError(SAXParseException e) throws SAXException {
        log(Logger.WARNING,
            new StringBuffer("Parsing Fatal Error: ")
                .append(e.getMessage( ))
                .toString( ));
        throw e;
    }

    private void log(int level, String msg) {
        if (logChannel != null) {
            logChannel.write(level, msg);
        }
    }
}
```

This example logs each error message to a logging facility and then passes on errors
and fatal errors to the wrapping application. Here's an example of setting an instance
of this error handler up for use—in this case for Zeus unmarshalling:

```
// Set the ErrorHandler on my unmarshaller class
EjbJarUnmarshaller.setErrorHandler(new EnhydraErrorHandler( ));

// Unmarshal into an object
EjbJar ejbJar = EjbJarUnmarshaller.unmarshal(myInputStream);
```

I'll deal with the specifics of this example as it applies to each data binding package
in later chapters. For now, you should see that a healthy knowledge of SAX makes
this a piece of cake.

Another important topic in data binding specifically related to SAX is entity resolution. When an XML document is read in, it often has a DOCTYPE statement, referring
to a DTD.

This statement could be a DTD on the network, as seen here:

```
<?xml version="1.0"?>

<!DOCTYPE ejb-jar
    PUBLIC '-//Sun Microsystems, Inc.//DTD Enterprise JavaBeans 1.1//EN'
          'http://java.sun.com/j2ee/dtds/ejb-jar_1_1.dtd'>
<ejb-jar>
  <description>
    The Account and Order EJBs represent a Customer and a
    Customer Order. Because these EJBs are dependent on each other to complete
    and manage an order(s) they are bundled together.
  </description>
  <display-name>Customer Component</display-name>
  <enterprise-beans>
    <entity>
      <!-- And so on... -->
    </entity>
  </enterprise-beans>
</ejb-jar>
```

This XML file refers to a DTD with a system ID of *http://java.sun.com/j2ee/dtds/ejb-jar_1_1.dtd.** During production, you would rarely want your well-tested application to have to access the network every time it unmarshals a file; to avoid this, you need to use an implementation of the SAX org.xml.sax.EntityResolver interface. This interface allows you to match the public and/or system ID of an entity (like that in the preceding XML file) and resolve it in a fashion of your choosing, instead of by the normal means. To give you an idea of how this works, Example 2-2 shows a class that resolves all references to the Sun EJB DTD at the URL shown above to a local copy of that DTD.

Example 2-2. Using an EntityResolver for Sun EJB DTDs

```
package javajaxb;

import java.io.File;
import java.io.FileInputStream;
import java.io.IOException;
import java.io.InputStream;

// SAX imports
import org.xml.sax.EntityResolver;
import org.xml.sax.InputSource;
import org.xml.sax.SAXException;

public class EjbDtdEntityResolver implements EntityResolver {
```

---

* If you're lost in the talk of system IDs, entities, and DOCTYPE declarations, I suggest you take a break from this book and pick up your copy of *XML in a Nutshell*. It will explain all of these concepts clearly. Then you can come back to this chapter and things will make more sense.

Example 2-2. Using an EntityResolver for Sun EJB DTDs (continued)

```
    private static final String EJB_DTD_SYSTEM_ID =
        "http://java.sun.com/j2ee/dtds/ejb-jar_1_1.dtd";

    private static final String EJB_DTD_LOCAL_ID =
        "/store/dtd/j2ee/ejb-jar_1_1.dtd";

    public InputSource resolveEntity(String publicID, String systemID)
        throws IOException, SAXException {

        if (systemID.equals(EJB_DTD_SYSTEM_ID)) {
            try {
                InputStream in =
                    new FileInputStream(new File(EJB_DTD_LOCAL_ID));
                return new InputSource(in);
            } catch (IOException e) {
                // use normal processing
                return null;
            }
        }

        // Not the DTD we care about, so perform normal processing
        return null;
    }
}
```

The resolveEntity() method is called when the DOCTYPE declaration is referenced:

```
    resolveEntity("-//Sun Microsystems, Inc.//DTD Enterprise JavaBeans 1.1//EN",
                  "http://java.sun.com/j2ee/dtds/ejb-jar_1_1.dtd");
```

By packaging a local copy of this DTD with your generated Java classes, you remove the need for a network connection and speed up the unmarshalling process. You would then register this with your unmarshalling code (shown here with the Castor API):

```
    Unmarshaller.setEntityResolver(new EjbDtdEntityResolver());
    EjbJar ejbJar = (EjbJar)Unmarshaller.unmarshal(myInputSource);
```

Again, I'll leave details of various implementations for later chapters, but a working knowledge of SAX can dramatically improve the quality and performance of your data binding code.

SAX is also an option, although not as compelling, for use in class generation. SAX cannot read DTDs, so it is not useful for generating Java classes from an XML DTD; however, it can be used to generate Java classes from XML Schemas or any other constraint model that follows the rules of the XML 1.0 specification. However, the process of building a set of Java classes often relies on hierarchical data (for example, seeing that a book element contains child elements named chapter, which in turn contain elements called section), which SAX isn't very helpful in providing. Because of this, data binding packages often use a modeled data approach, like that provided by DOM, JDOM, or dom4j. Some packages do use SAX, but end up building their own proprietary data structures. In these cases, I'm generally of the opinion that the standard model is better than a custom one. Additionally, the process of class generation is *almost always* done at compile time, when speed is less of an issue. This makes the use of a modeled data API even more attractive, as performance becomes less of an issue.

DOM

After you've made it past SAX, the next API to examine is DOM. DOM is not nearly as crucial a portion of most data binding packages, especially in comparison to SAX. However, for class generation, DOM is an attractive option. It offers an XML object model that is well documented and well understood, so it has shown up in many data binding frameworks. However, with the growing popularity of alternative models like JDOM and dom4j, DOM is now just one option among many for that layer of the data binding framework. Additionally, DOM implementations generally use SAX under the hood (as discussed in the last chapter). Because of this, you'll find the SAX concepts covered in this chapter important when dealing with DOM-based class generators.

From a more technical perspective, DOM can be handy for performing class generation tasks because of the maturity of the API. Because DOM has been around for such a long time (as compared to JDOM and dom4j), it has many support APIs that can be layered on top of it. For example, technologies like XPointer, XPath, and XLink allow you to find specific nodes very easily (in both the current and other documents). It's fairly easy to find implementations of all of these built on the DOM, while stable implementations for JDOM and dom4j are just not as common.* For these reasons, DOM can be an attractive solution for developers working on class generation and trying to bolster an existing implementation with helper APIs.

Dependent APIs

When it comes to business-centric APIs, the tables turn a bit. Instead of a data binding package relying on these APIs, higher-level APIs often rely on data binding. This makes sense, as all programming is simply a layering of code that moves from the very specific (shifting bits) to the very general (buying a DVD). I won't spend too much time in this section, as these APIs can change their use of data binding as quickly as I can write about them. I'll touch on only a few items and then move on to XML constraints

SOAP

SOAP is a perfect example of an API that can use data binding very naturally. Consider that the entire purpose of SOAP is to transfer information between systems. This data can be very complex though, and even user-defined.

---

* This doesn't mean that these implementations don't exist; it just means that they are not as common and generally not as well tested and documented

For example, here's a fairly basic SOAP response:

```
<SOAP-ENV:Envelope xmlns:SOAP-ENV="http://schemas.xmlsoap.org/soap/envelope/"
        SOAP-ENV:encodingStyle="http://schemas.xmlsoap.org/soap/encoding/"/>
  <SOAP-ENV:Body>
    <resp:stockQuoteResponse xmlns:resp="http://www.stockQuotes.com">
      <quote symbol="ALGX" name="Allegiance Telecom">
        <volume>2,964,600</volume>
        <averageVolume>924,318</averageVolume>
        <marketCap>411,700,000</marketCap>
      </quote>
    </resp:stockQuoteResponse>
  </SOAP-ENV:Body>
</SOAP-ENV:Envelope>
```

Don't get hung up in the envelope and header information; it's the body of the message that is interesting in relation to data binding. Because data has to be transferred via XML, data binding can offer a means of converting that data into XML. You can see that, in this case, the data is a stock quote.

Currently, most SOAP packages pick this data apart piece by piece and convert each to XML. However, consider that this same data could be represented just as well by a Java class like this:

```
public class Quote {
    private String symbol;
    private String name;
    private float volume;
    private float averageVolume;
    private long marketCap;

    public String getSymbol();
    public String getName();
    public float getVolume();
    public float getAverageVolume();
    public long getMarketCap();

    // Other mutator methods
}
```

Instead of having to work at this data piece by piece, the envelope of the SOAP message could be set as follows:

```
// Marshal (with data binding) quote object into XML
StringWriter stringWriter = new StringWriter();
currentStockQuote.marshal(stringWriter);

// Create the SOAP body
Body soapBody = new Body();
Vector bodyEntries = new Vector();
bodyEntries.add(stringWriter.toString());
soapBody.setBodyEntries(bodyEntries);

// Add the SOAP body
soapEnvelope.setBody(soapBody);
```

Here, rather than working through the Quote object piece by piece, data binding is used to write the object out to XML in a single simple line of code. Obviously, this is a case in which data binding can really shine. Currently, data binding isn't used too much in SOAP implementations, mostly due to the relative immaturity of both SOAP and data binding implementations. However, as both start to shore up and become more stable, and as custom types are used more often, expect data binding to become an alternative to tedious piecemeal data serialization.

UDDI

Another application in which data binding can help is a UDDI registry. In this case, custom data types are not as much of an issue, as the information stored in a UDDI registry is constant. Generally, a universal resource name (URN), category, access point, and possibly a WSDL file reference are stored for each web service registered with UDDI. However, this information is often persisted to an XML document for short-term storage (and later persisted to a database for long-term storage). In these cases, a simple RegisteredService could be created and stored in a Java list with other services, as part of a Registry object. I won't list the code for these generated objects here, as you should be starting to get the idea by now of how data-bound classes look.

In any case, with these sorts of objects, and persistence only a simple invocation of the marshal() method, programming tasks become very simple. I'm not going to spend a lot of time listing all the APIs in which data binding could be useful; you probably already have a few in mind that I haven't thought of. However, you should be clear that data binding is both incredibly useful for these higher-level APIs and simple to use. Data binding takes the complexity of reading and writing XML data out of APIs that should be focused on business rather than data tasks.

Constraint-Modeled Data

Once you've got a handle on the APIs involved with data binding (and those that could depend on it), you need to have a solid understanding of XML constraints. These constraints are one of the most important aspects of working with class generation (along with the binding schema), and your constraint model will dictate the classes that result. Good constraint modeling will result in efficient, business-oriented classes; however, poor modeling can result in hundreds of classes or convoluted names and methods.

One thing I do want to mention before diving into this section and the rest of the book is that I expect you to know the basics of DTDs and XML Schema. When I cover alternatives like Relax NG, I'll include some basic explanations related to the examples, but I don't want to spend time covering syntax of DTDs and schemas. There are plenty of available books on the subject, so you may want to have one or more of these handy as you work through the examples. I'm also going to assume that you can pick up some skills by following along with the examples; in other words, I'm not going to spend a lot of time talking about constraint basics, except those that relate specifically to data binding. Hopefully seeing lots of DTDs and schemas in this book will make you examine how you write your own constraints and pick up some good ideas. That said, let me dive into specific constraint models and what to watch for when writing constraints for use in data binding class generation.

DTDs

Currently, DTDs are the basis of most data binding packages. DTDs were defined in the XML 1.0 specification, and you can learn about their syntax and limitations in O'Reilly's *Learning XML* or *XML in a Nutshell*. DTDs are not as expressive as many other constraint models, like XML Schema or Relax NG, but they remain the core of XML constraints. Tens of thousands, if not hundreds of thousands, of DTDs are used in production today. Because of this, even if you don't ever plan to write a DTD, you'll need to understand them and how to structure them for efficient data binding use.

First, use clear and concise names for your elements and attributes. This is true for any constraint model. Naming an element cfm for "Container Field Mapping" might seem like a great typing shortcut, until you use the generated classes from that DTD:

```
// It's unclear what this class is, or does!
CFM cfm = new CFM( );
```

Suddenly, that savings in typing doesn't seem like such a good idea. Consider the more verbose, but clearer, name containerFieldMapping:

```
// The purpose of this class is much clearer
ContainerFieldMapping mapping = new ContainerFieldMapping( );
```

One limitation of DTDs is that they do not support namespaces. Because of this, you may have to think a more about the names of elements that serve different purposes, but might otherwise have the same name. In other words, two elements with the same name cannot have different definitions. Consider the following XML document fragment:

```
<store>
  <inventory>
    <item id="lotr-438-1">
      <price>39.99</price>
    </item>
    <item id="wot-980-3">
      <price>44.99</price>
    </item>
  </inventory>

  <equipment>
    <item model="cr122-a" quantity="9">Cash Register</item>
    <item model="as-599" quanity="129">Book shelf</item>
  </equipment>
</store>
```

The element name item means different things in these two contexts. You would not want the first item elements to specify a model attribute, but you would also not want the latter item elements to specify an id value. In other words, these two elements, named the same, represent two different data types. Using namespaces, you could distinguish them from each other; however, in a DTD-based environment, this isn't possible. As a result, you'll need to use two different data types and, thus, two different element names. You might use inventoryItem or equipmentItem, or something altogether different, to ensure you don't have name collisions in your DTD.

Finally, I want to make one other general, change-your-life type of suggestion: design your constraints before your documents. I realize that for most of you, the process consists of writing an XML file and then using some tool to generate a DTD from it. When you just need a quick solution, this approach probably works out well. However, for longer-term solutions and situations in which you want to use data binding, writing the document first is a pretty bad idea. You end up forgetting to add an attribute, forgetting to think about this special case or that exceptional condition, or forgetting that you duplicated names. You end up going back and changing the DTD, over and over again. The result is you haven't really defined constraints; you wouldn't be changing them if you did. Instead, you developed a model, and that model is an ever-changing thing. Your generated classes from a week ago are no longer compatible with those developed yesterday, and those you developed yesterday probably won't work with those you'll generate a week later. The result is the mess you see in Figure 2-1.

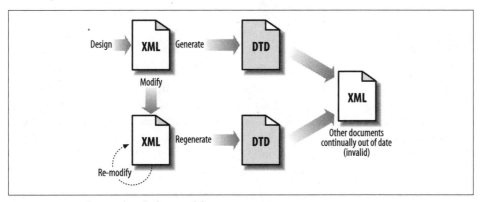

Figure 2-1. Developing data before modeling constraints

This mess occurs because you write specific data first, and then you write constraints to fit that specific data. You are not thinking about the whole set of data you need to represent and then developing a model. In other words, you want to develop a general solution that your specific data fits, not the other way around. This results in a process flow like that shown in Figure 2-2, which is much different than Figure 2-1.

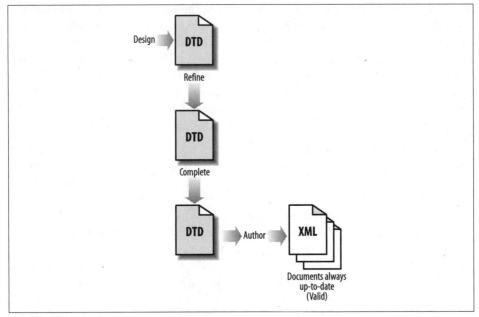

Figure 2-2. Modeling constraints before data

Even though constraint models like XML Schema offer you richer syntax, namespaces and a wealth of other options, following these simple guidelines will help when dealing with schemas as well.

XML Schema

I want to specifically address XML Schema because for most data binding packages, it's the second constraint model that is supported. In the chapters on specific data binding frameworks, I detail what each project supports, but while you are reading this, expect most open source alternatives to JAXB to contain XML Schema support. Because of this, you should start thinking about how you're going to use schemas, as they do offer nice features not found in DTDs.

First, when using XML Schema, you'll want to consider using namespaces. Namespaces can solve the naming collisions mentioned in the DTD section. However, you should spend some time learning how your specific data binding package handles namespaces. Some packages ignore them completely, which doesn't help you out at all. Some assign different Java packages based on the namespaces, which is helpful, but in some cases not desirable (in other words, it's a good option, but is preferably configurable). Others allow you to map the names or use prefixes—as you can see, there are a lot of different handling approaches. You'll want to understand this handling thoroughly before using namespaces, or you may end up with results you weren't expecting or desiring.

Another XML Schema feature you'll want to take heavy advantage of is the type safety that schemas provide. In DTDs, you can specify character data only for textual content (PCDATA and CDATA). As a result, you'll need to rely on binding schemas when using DTDs to provide type mappings. However, schemas allow types like integer or string in the constraint model; these types all have analogs in Java and therefore can help ensure that your XML data matches the types you want to use in Java. You'll also want to leave room for growth in these types; I've often seen an integer used without thought when a float was actually required for long-term needs. This leads back to the process shown in Figure 2-1, requiring changes that invalidate earlier versions of generated classes as well as XML documents. As always, spend plenty of time planning your constraints and making sure that they work not only for your current data, but also for future data.

And More ...

Although DTDs and XML Schema hold the majority of developers' attention, I'd be remiss in not mentioning some of the alternatives that are growing in popularity. XML Schema interest is largely driven by the recognition of DTD limitations. However, the XML Schema specification is extremely complex, and many developers are interested in only 15 or 20 percent of the features in the specification. As a result, a lot of weight is carried around by parsers is never used. This has driven several efforts to develop a schema-like constraint language without all the complexity of XML Schema.

What seems to be the best alternative is Relax NG, hosted by OASIS at *http://www. oasis-open.org/committees/relax-ng* (which is aliased to *http://www.relaxng.org*). This is the result of two constraint models, Relax and Trex, joining forces and creating a new option for constraint representation. To see what Relax NG looks like, consider the following XML document:

```
<?xml version="1.0"?>

<addressBook>
  <card>
    <givenName>John</givenName>
    <familyName>Smith</familyName>
    <email>js@example.com</email>
  </card>
  <card>
    <name>Fred Bloggs</name>
    <email>fb@example.net</email>
  </card>
</addressBook>
```

Here's a sample of a Relax NG schema from the Relax NG tutorial:

```
<?xml version="1.0"?>

<element name="addressBook" xmlns="http://relaxng.org/ns/structure/0.9">
  <zeroOrMore>
```

```
        <element name="card">
          <choice>
            <element name="name">
              <text/>
            </element>
            <group>
              <element name="givenName">
                <text/>
              </element>
              <element name="familyName">
                <text/>
              </element>
            </group>
          </choice>
          <element name="email">
            <text/>
          </element>
          <optional>
            <element name="note">
              <text/>
            </element>
          </optional>
        </element>
      </zeroOrMore>
    </element>
```

Here, I've specified the allowed elements, detailed which ones can have text, and specified which elements are optional. If you've ever looked at an XML Schema, this should look somewhat familiar; however, it's vastly simpler than the same constraints in an XML Schema, which I don't include here because it took more than a hundred lines! In any case, this is a simple, intuitive solution that has a lot of programmers pretty excited.

Currently, Relax NG is in early stages of activity, as is support for it in parsers and processors. That said, it will only increase in popularity as developers want a simpler option than XML Schema provides. The backing of the specification by OASIS, a recognized standards body, will also aid in its adoption. Currently, no data binding packages support Relax NG; however, open source packages like Castor and Zeus are likely to offer support for Relax NG if their communities desire it (early indications indicate this could be a very popular feature). I'd keep an eye on this, as it will certainly show up in later versions of data binding frameworks (as well as later editions of this book, I'd bet).

API Transparence

Before wrapping up on theory and concepts, I wanted to dive into some theoretical issues; don't worry, I'll keep it short and to the point! The issues I want to address relate to *API transparence*. When using data binding, you actually spend very little time working directly with the data binding API itself; instead, you work with classes generated by the API. Because of that, these generated classes become critical to your applications. However, when an API severs itself from the classes it generates, you can run into all sorts of nasty problems.

 Actually, the API only *appears* to sever itself in many cases. In other words, many frameworks generate classes with methods like this:

```
public static EjbJar unmarshal(InputStream inputStream)
    throws IOException {
    return (EjbJar)Unmarshaller
        .unmarshal(inputStream, EjbJar.class);
}
```

As you can see, the method on the generated class simply hides the details of using the API from your programs. However, from your application's point of view, you aren't interfacing with the data binding API in your code.

Independence

The first thing you'll want to make note of is the level of independence your generated classes offer you. In other words, are you tethered to the data binding API at runtime once classes are generated? Or do your classes run without ever using that API? The latter case is referred to as *API independence*. Obviously, the fewer dependencies your generated classes have, the easier deployment becomes.

Another question to ask is that of *version independence*: do your classes have to use a specific version of SAX, a vendor's parser, or your data binding framework? These are all critical questions and can cause bugs that are extremely tricky to track down. Like packaging up your data binding framework (if your generated classes require them), you'll need to supply appropriate versions of SAX, parsers, and other APIs, if your framework requires them at runtime. By knowing the answers to these questions, you'll not only be prepared to use a data binding framework, but also to deploy the solutions it creates. In fact, each issue deserves a detailed look, given here.

API independence

First, you need to find out what dependencies your generated classes have at runtime, when the classes are put into action. This will vary from framework to framework, and sometimes with the options you have set in each framework. For example, JAXB requires that the JAXB API (the actual *jar* archive) be in the classpath at runtime for marshalling and unmarshalling. Castor and Coins are in the same category; however, Zeus generates classes that don't require anything but a SAX XML parser for marshalling and unmarshalling. Whichever package you choose, you'll want to deploy the correct packages and *jars* at runtime to avoid ugly ClassNotFoundExceptions.

I recommend considering deploying your data binding API and related classes into your runtime classpath, even if they aren't required. While your generated classes may not need them, you'll often find handy utilities in these frameworks. For example, some basic `ErrorHandler` or `EntityResolver` implementations may be included in a data binding framework, as well as parsing tools to make common XML handling tasks easier. That also prevents any errors from occurring, which saves you from remembering which framework produces independent classes and which don't.

Version independence

Another issue, and one that is even more important, is versioning. Not specific to data binding, versioning is always a bit of a pain to work with. Your generated classes will almost always outlast a specific version of a framework, and you'll want to try your hardest to always keep up-to-date on API releases. In general, as long as method signatures don't change, things will work out alright. In other words, if your API developers are doing their jobs, you're going to have code that works with any version of its related data binding API. However, depending on other developers isn't always the best way to guarantee stress-free evenings. To ensure that a new version of an API works with your classes, you should compile your generated classes (or recompile, actually) using the new version of your framework. I highly recommend testing by unmarshalling from XML and then marshalling back to XML, using the most complex XML instance documents you have on hand. If these basic tests pass, you're going to be OK 99 times out of 100.

As for the other one time, it usually crops up when you begin using an XML document that has some piece of data in it that you've never run across before, such as special characters, or contains data that isn't used in your other existing documents. Since this isn't a case you can specifically test for (you're always going to miss something), careful error handling in your application code is your best bet. Getting an odd `NullPointerException` or a `SealingViolation` results in confusion, but provides almost nothing to go on in terms of tracking down bugs. However, using a good SAX `ErrorHandler` that traps errors, obtains line numbers, and writes out something useful (like "SAX Parsing Error on Line 25: error in handling 'type' attribute") is perfect for debugging problems that crop up with new versions of frameworks.

Integration

The next subject is *API integration*. This term refers to integration with your application and other unrelated APIs. In other words, how well does the code generated by a data binding framework work and play with your own code? More often than not, the generated classes are normal Java classes; however, integration takes things a step further. For example, can you have meaningful error messages reported in a format compatible with the rest of your application? The answer should be "yes." For example, you want to ensure that generated classes are in a format you can live with; this may involve the names of methods, as well as the types used for multiple-valued properties. Some applications may work best with typed arrays (like `Person[]`), while others may work better with Java collections (`Lists` and `Maps`). There isn't a right or wrong solution, as your application will determine your needs at a specific time.

In all of these cases, as you may have guessed, the key is flexibility. Your framework should allow as much flexibility as possible, through binding schemas or any other facility. That could mean you could opt to ignore certain methods, specify packages, generate (or not generate) interfaces versus concrete classes, or use typed arrays versus Java collection classes. What you don't want is an API that gives you one choice for all situations; you'll almost certainly find your application needs a different choice (usually right after you've selected the framework!). In any event, this is a case in which you want a long laundry list of useful features and goodies supported by your data binding framework of choice.

Interoperation

The final aspect of data binding I want to address is *API interoperation*. This refers to your data binding framework (Castor, for example) being able to interoperate with another (let's say JAXB). For many developers, the importance of this aspect of APIs is vastly undervalued. The prevailing mentality is "We chose this framework, so who cares if it works with other frameworks." However, that attitude ignores the fact that, more often than not, frameworks, APIs, and vendors change more often than developers' resumes these days. Time and time again, I've seen hundreds, thousands, or millions of lines of code thrown out because management dictates a change in a framework, vendor, or product. In these cases, interoperation becomes a huge factor, and one that can save weeks of work in retooling code.

In the case of data binding frameworks, you shouldn't be concerned with the actual methods used to generate classes; these are fire-and-forget tasks, as once the classes are generated, they're ready for use. The same is true for constraint models; if you use DTDs, they should work with any framework that supports that constraint model. The same goes for XML Schema, Relax NG, or anything else. This does become a factor, though, in two specific areas: the binding schema and in marshalling and unmarshalling.

The first case involves how XML documents and constraints are mapped to Java; if this is vastly different from framework to framework, the resulting Java classes and data are not going to be compatible, and all of that rework I just mentioned kicks into gear. However, if binding schemas work across packages (even with minor changes), then if you do need to change APIs, you're fairly well protected.

The second case involves the generated classes; if marshalling and unmarshalling is significantly different, you will need to regenerate all of your classes to work with a new framework; and that means bugs, bugs, bugs. The ability to use the classes generated from one framework with another framework is invaluable here and this brings us back to API independence, mentioned not so long ago (remember?). If your generated classes don't depend on *any* API, then you're off to a good start in this area.

Unfortunately, advancements in this area are few and far between, at best. All major APIs have developed their own format for binding schemas and their own dependencies for generated classes, and things aren't (yet) getting much better. That said, as Sun's JAXB specification firms up, you should expect to see some convergence. Zeus, for example, uses a binding schema that is a superset of the JAXB schema in most regards, meaning that the two are nearly interchangeable (the definition of "nearly" depending on how many Zeus-specific features you use). You should expect to see similar steps taken with Castor's mapping file as well, bringing all these APIs into better states of interoperation.

That said, we're done with theory (at least for a while). I hope you made it through these paragraphs, as I'll refer to these terms quite a bit, especially when comparing APIs in later chapters. Additionally, it should have really whet your appetite for some code and juicy technical meat. That's great, of course, because the next chapter is going to be full of it. I'll show you how to generate Java classes from your XML constraints, and things will become fun. Hold on, and let's get to it.

CHAPTER 3

Generating Classes

Now that we're through the formalities, I want to focus specifically on the JAXB data binding framework. In this chapter, I start by discussing how to take a set of XML constraints and convert those constraints to a set of Java source files. In addition to seeing how this work with JAXB, this chapter should give you a solid idea of how class generation works so that when we move to other frameworks (in the second half of this book), you'll already have a handle on class generation and how it works. I also briefly touch on the future of JAXB—specifically, which constraint models are supported and which should be supported in future versions.

 Without belaboring the point, I want to be clear that this and other JAXB chapters were written using a prerelease version of Sun's JAXB framework (the 1.0 version was not yet available). Because of this, small inconsistencies may creep in as this book goes to press. If you run across a problem with the examples, consult the JAXB documentation and feel free to contact us. Details of who to send mail to are in the preface of the book, and you can also check the book's web site at *http://www.newInstance.com*.

Process Flow

First, let's run through the process flow involved with generating constraints. This will help you get an idea of where we're going and how the pieces in this chapter fit together. It should also form a simple mental checklist for you to follow when generating classes; if you skip a step, problems crop up, so be sure to take each in turn. Here's how the steps break down:

1. Create a set of constraints for your XML data.
2. Create a binding schema for converting the constraints into Java.
3. Generate the classes using the binding framework.
4. Compile the classes and ensure they are ready for use.

I'll cover each step in order.

Constraints

The first step is to create a set of constraints for your XML data. If you followed my advice from Chapter 2, then you are doing this *before* writing your XML documents. That tends, as I mentioned, to produce more organized constraint models. You'll want to ensure that your constraint model is complete, as well; the last thing you want is to have to add an attribute or element that you forgot and then regenerate your source files. As mentioned previously, this can cause conflicts with older versions of generated classes conflicting with your updated ones.

Additionally, now you need to ensure that your constraint model syntax is supported by the binding framework you want to use. In other words, if you go to a lot of trouble to generate a documented XML Schema and then find out that your framework of choice supports only DTDs, expect some yelling and screaming. Take the time *before* writing constraints to verify this, or you can't say that I didn't warn you when things get ugly. As a general rule, you will never go wrong using DTDs right now, as all frameworks support them. I'd guess that a year or two from now, XML Schemas will be just as safe, but the frameworks simply aren't there yet.

Once you've developed your constraints, you need to perform some level of testing before you run your class generation tools on them. This is a crucial step, as it verifies that your data is going to match up with your constraints. Write several XML documents (or use existing ones, if you have them already) and validate them against your new constraints. This can be done with Xerces, your favorite XML parser, or various IDEs available for XML authoring. You'll want to try and test as many different documents as you can, preferably with a variety of data in them. Testing many different documents is the best way to make sure you didn't misname or leave something out, which would cause problems down the line. Once you've got the verified constraint model and are happy with it, you're ready to move on to a binding schema.

 You should realize that documentation and comments in your DTD or constraint model will not affect class generation. Hopefully that doesn't urge you to leave documentation out but pushes you to write well-formatted comments. This will help your co-workers and generally make life easier. So please, comment, comment, comment.

Binding Schema

Once you've got your constraint set ready, you'll need to write a binding schema for most frameworks. There is a lot of variance from the simplest binding schema to the most complex, so don't expect me to cover all the details of binding schemas here, or even in this chapter. I'll explain the basic options in this chapter and then devote Chapter 6 to a complete exploration of the topic. You will get a taste of what's to come in this chapter, though.

You'll notice that I put a qualifier on the first sentence of that last paragraph: *most* frameworks. Some data binding frameworks do not require a binding schema, although they may allow more advanced options through the use of one. Currently, JAXB requires a binding schema, but Castor and Zeus do not. The Coins framework uses a significantly different process, but does employ the idea of a binding schema. So while you may always provide a binding schema for the sake of specifying options, realize that you don't have to in some cases.

Binding schemas provide the ability to specify both local and global options, and this concept is important to grasp. For example, specifying the Java package to generate source code within is a global option and affects all generated code. However, supplying a class name of Employee for the XML element person is a local option and applies only to that element. You'll want to be very careful when setting global options, as every generated class is affected. Of course, some frameworks allow you to override global options for specific elements, so you often get the best of both worlds.

Finally, you need to know the format that your framework uses for binding schemas. As I already mentioned, this is generally some XML-compliant format. The elements and attributes allowed by each framework often varies, though; be sure to use the correct conventions for the correct framework. As JAXB standardizes, expect to see binding schema syntax to converge on what JAXB uses, but for now things are still a bit spread out across various frameworks. Once you've developed your binding schema, though, you can pass it along with your constraints and wait for the magic to happen.

Generation

At this point, the actual mechanics of class generation kick in. This is generally a sort of "black box," as frameworks each approach this step of the process differently. You supply a set of constraints, usually a binding schema, and out pops a set of source code ready for compilation. Because JAXB is closed source and the code is not available for viewing, I'm not going to get into specifics of how JAXB's black box works. In the chapters for the open source frameworks, I will address these details, but for JAXB, just trust the framework to do that hard work.

Source Code

The result of the generation step is one or more Java source files. These files should be ready for compilation, using normal Java approaches (javac). At this point, frameworks generally leave you on your own, assuming you can compile these classes to a directory and location of your choice. Be sure to use the -d switch (on javac) so that any package you specified is built into the output location of your compiled classes.

What About Multithreading?

This book focuses mainly on how to use data binding APIs and therefore doesn't spend much time on issues like threading, locking, and multiprocessing. However, for those of you who are wondering, here's a short look at how multithreading affects data binding.

It is important to realize that class generation does not make any changes to either your constraint model or your binding schema; these can be used repeatedly without any problem. However, like XML parsers, you'll want to avoid trying to process these documents (the constraints and binding schema) with multiple processes simultaneously. This is a basic I/O principle, but is always worth saying for those of you getting a little overzealous with threading. It also brings up another important concept: compile-time class generation. While it's certainly possible to generate classes from constraints at runtime, it isn't a very good idea unless you're writing a data binding tool. While it's possible to shove the generated source code into a javac process and then even hook a Java ClassLoader into the resultant classes, this is really not a good idea. I highly recommend generating source at compile time, compiling these files, and then using them at runtime, in the plain-vanilla standard Java approach.

 There are a few odd cases in which data binding packages generate source code that will not compile. This is almost always the result of a bug in the data binding implementation, rather than something you have done incorrectly. I'll address some of these cases in the text, but if you see this occurring, you should report your problem to the mailing list for the framework being used.

Keep in mind, though, that this source code may not be in a pretty, formatted, commented state (as all the rest of your code is, right?). This means that Javadoc and other documentation methods on these classes will be terse, if not nonexistent. Hopefully this will change as frameworks get the basics down and move on to finer details like this. Additionally, the generated classes will almost always be dependant on one another, and will need to be compiled at the same time. Once you've got a set of Java classes, simply add them to your classpath, and you are ready to use them.

Once you've put all of this into one coherent process, the result is similar to that shown in Figure 3-1. Even if you are using a framework other than JAXB, this process will be similar for any class generation setup.

Creating the Constraints

The first step in getting ready for class generation, as you can see from Figure 3-1, is getting a set of constraints ready to generate classes from. As this isn't a book on writing XML (and there are plenty of good ones on the subject already), I'm not going to spend time describing how to formulate constraints.

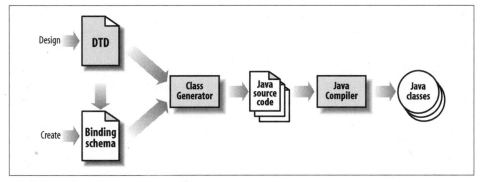

Figure 3-1. Class generation process flow

I'll assume that you're capable of figuring out how you want your data represented and then using DTDs or schemas or your constraint model of choice to describe that data. I do want to touch on a few points relevant to data binding, and JAXB specifically, though, and then provide several DTDs for working through the examples.

JAXB and DTDs

First, as I've mentioned several times, JAXB currently supports only DTDs. From what I can gather from the specification, newsgroups, and mailing lists, this is the plan all the way through the 1.0 final version of the specification and framework. There is a lot of momentum to follow up this release with a "version.next" that does support XML Schema, though.* JAXB does support all the features of DTDs, so you should be able to use any DTDs you've already developed for your data binding needs.

To get started, I want to present a simple DTD that I'll use as a starting point for most of the rest of this chapter. Example 3-1 shows that DTD, which represents a simple movie database.†

Example 3-1. Movie database DTD

```
<!ELEMENT movies (movie+)>
<!ATTLIST movies
          version    CDATA    #REQUIRED
>
```

---

* I realize that for some of you, this may seem contradictory to what you've heard. Early on in the JAXB effort (back in the "codename: Adelard" days, there was a lot of talk about XML Schema support in the first version. That talk died off, though, as getting out even a DTD version began to take more time. In other words, deadlines slipped and things changed.

† Occasionally, folks ask me why I don't use more realistic examples like a telecommunications PoP configuration file, a financial planning package (in XML), or something similar. These examples rarely make sense unless you're in those particular industries, so I chose examples that don't require special knowledge of a specific industry.

Example 3-1. Movie database DTD (continued)

```
<!ELEMENT movie (title, cast, director?, producer*)>

<!ELEMENT cast (actor+)>
<!ELEMENT title (#PCDATA)>
<!ELEMENT director (#PCDATA)>
<!ELEMENT producer (#PCDATA)>

<!ELEMENT actor (#PCDATA)>
<!ATTLIST actor
                headliner    (true | false)    'false'
>
```

Do I Really Have to Type This in?

Since most of you are busy writing your own code and don't want to type the examples in by hand, they are all available for download from this book's web site, *http://www.newInstance.com*. Navigate to the Writing link, click the cover for this book, and you'll be able to read updates on the book; download the DTDs, XML documents, binding schemas, and Java classes from the examples, and find other supplemental material. You'll also learn about new editions, extra goodies found only online, and more, so check it out.

This is pretty basic stuff; just so you get an idea of how this looks when presented as data, Example 3-2 shows an XML document that conforms to this DTD.

Example 3-2. Sample movie database

```
<?xml version="1.0" encoding="UTF-8"?>
<!DOCTYPE movies SYSTEM "movies.dtd">

<movies version="1.1">
  <movie>
    <title>Pitch Black</title>
    <cast>
      <actor headliner="true">Vin Diesel</actor>
      <actor headliner="true">Radha Mitchell</actor>
      <actor>Vic Wilson</actor>
    </cast>
    <producer>Tom Engelman</producer>
  </movie>
  <movie>
    <title>Memento</title>
    <cast>
      <actor headliner="true">Guy Pearce</actor>
      <actor headliner="true">Carrie-Anne Moss</actor>
    </cast>
    <director>Christopher Nolan</director>
```

Example 3-2. Sample movie database (continued)

```
  <producer>Suzanne Todd</producer>
  <producer>Jennifer Todd</producer>
 </movie>
</movies>
```

There isn't anything remarkable here; I've simply illustrated what XML looks like in relation to its constraints. Before moving on to binding schemas, though, there are a few more things to point out.

Deterministic Modeling

First on the list of important considerations is *determinism* in your models. I know that sounds like something you'd hear in a political speech, but it is pretty important. Determinism is a fancy word for unambiguous and basically means that your constraint cannot be misinterpreted or interpreted as more than one possibility. If a particular constraint cannot be interpreted without looking ahead or could also fulfill another model, it is *nondeterministic*. For example (from the XML recommendation):

```
  <!ELEMENT non-deterministic ((b, c) | (b, d))>
```

Here, if a b element is encountered, it's not clear whether a parser should expect a c or a d element to follow it. This would require the parser to read ahead and therefore is nondeterministic. To fix this problem, you would collapse the declaration to:

```
  <!ELEMENT deterministic (b, (c | d))>
```

This also illustrates an important point: generally, changing a nondeterministic model into a deterministic one. Nondeterminism is a pain to deal with when you're trying to validate XML; it's flat-out impossible to deal with in data binding. The class generation tools will either completely choke or produce all sorts of wild results (try it sometime; it's actually sort of fun!). Generally, XML IDEs will catch this, but you'll want to watch for this problem, as it creates uncertain results and is a nonobvious problem for constraints to have.

Simple Elements

Another thing to think about when defining your constraints is *simple element* definitions. A simple element is an element that has only textual content. Its model looks like this:

```
  <!ELEMENT title (#PCDATA)>
  <!ELEMENT director (#PCDATA)>
```

Both elements are simple and contain only PCDATA (parsed character data). So, in generated classes, you might expect to do something like this:

```
  String movieTitle = movie.getTitle();
  String director = movie.getDirector();
```

However, this isn't the case. JAXB and other data binding frameworks are going to generate classes for your elements in the general case. There are ways to get around this, and I'll cover them in the chapter on binding schemas, but in the simplest case, you will need to write code that looks more like this:

```
Title titleObject = movie.getTitle( );
String movieTitle = titleObject.getValue( );

Director directorObject = movie.getDirector( );
String director = directorObject.getValue( );
```

As you can see, more of an object hierarchy is built than you might have expected. Of course, you could use the first version of the code if you changed the constraints to look like this:

```
<!ELEMENT movies (movie+)>
<!ATTLIST movies
          version   CDATA    #REQUIRED
>

<!ELEMENT movie (cast, producer*)>
<!ATTLIST movie
          title    CDATA    #REQUIRED
          director CDATA    #IMPLIED
>

<!ELEMENT cast (actor+)>
<!ELEMENT producer (#PCDATA)>

<!ELEMENT actor (#PCDATA)>
<!ATTLIST actor
                headliner    (true | false)    'false'
>
```

Here, I've collapsed these two simple elements into attributes on the movie element; the result is that they are generated as simple Java Strings and available through accessor methods on the generated Movie object. This can be extended into a more general principle: elements are turned into Java objects and attributes are turned into Java member variables (usually Java primitives like int, float, String, etc.). Here's the resultant object:

```
public class Movie {
    private String title;
    private String director;
    // Other variables

    public String getTitle( ) {
        return title;
    }

    public String getDirector( ) {
        return director;
    }
```

```
    // Other accessor and mutator methods...
}
```

The result is a much easier object to use. The moral of this little tale is that well-designed constraints can result in cleaner and easier-to-use generated objects. It also results in better XML design, as now single values are stored as XML attributes, with multiple values stored in XML elements.

However, you should be careful not to get too overzealous in this collapsing of simple elements. For example, you might look at the producer element and thinking you can collapse it into the movie element as an attribute as well. However, you'd end up with a different constraint model; you would be able to specify only one producer, instead of more than one, as desired. In this case, it's appropriate to have a separate producer element, since that element can occur multiple times within the movie element. You're going to end up with a list of producers in your code:

```
// Using Java collections...
List producerList = movie.getProducerList();

// or, possibly...
Producer[] producerArray = movie.getProducer();
```

Be careful not to go crazy with this approach, or you'll end up changing the constraint set itself, rather than just "enhancing" the one that you already have.

Constraint Naming

A final consideration in constraint modeling: be careful of the names that you use. Remember that in data binding, your generated classes are going to use names defined in your DTD. Take this DTD fragment for part of a role-playing game's descriptor, for example:

```
<!ELEMENT characters (character+)>

<!ELEMENT character EMPTY>
<!ATTLIST character
          name    CDATA   #REQUIRED
          race    (human | elf | dwarf | orc) #REQUIRED
          class   (paladin | knight | mage | archer) #REQUIRED
>
```

This looks pretty innocent, until you run JAXB's class generation tool and end up with this source file fragment:

```
public class Character {
    // Normal variables and methods

    public String getClass() {
        return _Class;
    }
}
```

Obviously, I've simplified things a bit, but you can see immediately that this is not a class that will compile; if you know much about Java, you'll realize that getClass() is a method on java.lang.Object that cannot be overridden (it's declared final).

If you tried to compile the resultant classes, you'd get an error like this:

```
Character.java:51: getClass() in Character cannot override getClass() in
    java.lang.Object; overridden method is final
    public String getClass() {
                   ^
1 error
```

You would either need to rename the attribute in your DTD or use a binding schema to map the class attribute to a different variable name in Java.

Now, I want to issue a warning here, before you change all of our DTDs to use Java-compliant names. If the data you are describing is best named class, string, or any other reserved word in Java, *leave the name alone!* However, if you can more accurately name a piece of data by using a nonreserved word, then it's a good idea to take these steps now before doing any class generation.

The point I'm trying to make is that you should use the best names possible for your constraints, but you should *not* make decisions about your data based on the possibility that the data may be used by JAXB or any other data binding framework. You'll just want to make a note to yourself of any names that could cause trouble and be sure to map those names to legal Java ones (I'll cover this in detail in Chapter 6).

Binding Schema Basics

Once you've got your constraints (I saved my movie database DTD as *movies.dtd*), you're ready to create a binding schema for your classes. This will instruct the class generation tool to generate classes, to use a specific Java package, to use collections, and a variety of other options. Although I won't spend a lot of time on the schemas in this chapter, I'll give you some basics that will get us through some simple examples. Specifically, I'll deal with global options here and leave the local options, as well as more advanced features, to Chapter 6.

The Minimum Binding Schema

The first thing that you'll want to get a handle on is the "minimum binding schema." This is the least-amount-of-work principle; often, you'll want to generate classes from your DTD without any changes. To do this, you'll need to create a binding schema that provides very minimal information to the JAXB schema compiler tool.

The JAXB binding schema is an XML document, and the root element must be xml-java-binding-schema. It must also have a single attribute, version, and currently the only allowed value for this attribute is 1.0-ea.[*]

 The JAXB download comes with the DTD for this schema. It's located in the [jaxb-root]/doc/ directory and called xjs.dtd.

For a minimal binding schema, you must specify the root element of the DTD being passed in; this allows JAXB to determine which generated object (in source code) is the "top-level" one. This is accomplished through the element element (yup, you read that right). By supplying the root attribute and giving it a value of true, you've given JAXB what it needs. Add to this the name attribute, which identifies the element you're working on and, finally, the type attribute, which tells JAXB what type of Java construct to create from the element. For the movies element, you want a Java class, so use the class value for this attribute.

That idea took a paragraph to explain, but requires only three or four lines to put into action. Example 3-3 shows a binding schema for the movie database DTD.

Example 3-3. Binding schema for movie database

```
<?xml version="1.0"?>

<xml-java-binding-schema version="1.0-ea">
  <element name="movies" type="class" root="true"/>
</xml-java-binding-schema>
```

Save this schema as *movies.xjs*. The standard extension for binding schemas in JAXB is *xjs*, and I'd recommend you use it as well. With this fairly small XML file, you're ready for basic data binding.

It is possible to perform basic class generation without a binding schema. The JAXB schema compiler allows you to specify the root element (or elements) on the command line to the compiler. I'm not a big fan of this approach, though, as it's impossible for another developer to know what you provided. In other words, the binding schema provides documentation about what options were used in class generation. For that reason, I encourage you to use the simple binding schema shown above, rather than the command-line options, for generating classes.

Global Options

In addition to specifying the root element, a few other basic options are worth pointing out now. These are all global options, meaning that they affect all generated

---

[*] Presumably, other values will be allowed when subsequent versions of the binding schema are released.

classes. You will need to use the `options` element, which is a child of the top-level `xml-java-binding-schema` element, to specify these. Each option has an attribute on that element, and you give a value for the property you want to set. These global options and the attributes used to set them are summarized in Table 3-1.

Table 3-1. Global binding schema options

Attribute name	Allowed values	Default	Purpose
`package`	Any legal package name	N/A	Sets the Java package that source files use (e.g., `com.oreilly.jaxb`)
`default-reference-collection-type`	`array`, `list`	`list`	Sets the default collection type for multiple-valued properties
`property-get-set-prefixes`	`true`, `false`	`true`	Indicates if the accessor and mutator methods generated have a get and set prefix (e.g., `getTitle( )` versus `title( )`)
`marshallable`	`true`, `false`	`true`	Indicates whether this class should have a `marshal( )` method generated
`unmarshallable`	`true`, `false`	`true`	Indicates whether this class should have an `unmarshal( )` method generated

As you can see, these options are generally pretty self-explanatory. For example, to generate the movies database classes within the `javajaxb.generated.movies` package, with all other options set to the default values, you'd use the binding schema shown in Example 3-4.

Example 3-4. Modified binding schema for movies database

```
<?xml version="1.0"?>

<xml-java-binding-schema version="1.0-ea">
  <options package="javajaxb.generated.movies" />

  <element name="movies" type="class" root="true"/>
</xml-java-binding-schema>
```

Pretty simple, isn't it? The resultant classes are all in the specified package. In this example, I've added in the specification to generate multiple-valued properties as arrays instead of Java lists:

```
    <?xml version="1.0"?>

    <xml-java-binding-schema version="1.0-ea">
      <options package="javajaxb.generated.movies"
               default-reference-collection-type="array" />

      <element name="movies" type="class" root="true"/>
    </xml-java-binding-schema>
```

The result of this addition is apparent in the Movies class, which has multiple Movie subobjects. The methods generated look like this (using arrays):

```
public Movie[] getMovie( ) {
    // implementation
}

public void setMovie(Movie[] _Movie) {
    // implementation
}
```

 I realize that to many of you, the name getMovie( ) may seem a bit odd. This is true for almost all programmers getting into data binding. While you'll learn how to change this method name in Chapter 6, you should be aware that many frameworks (including some covered in this book) use this same sort of naming schema. It's not pretty, but you might want to start getting used to it.

Without using this property, Java collection classes are used, and the same method looks like this in the generated source code:

```
public List getMovie( ) {
    // implementation
}

public void deleteMovie( ) {
    // implementation
}

public void emptyMovie( ) {
    // implementation
}
```

As you can see, there is both a different return value from the getMovie() method, as well as a few new methods added, specific to Java List types. One other thing to notice is that there isn't a setMovie(List movie) method. To change the movies list, you'll need to write code like this:

```
// Obtain the current list
List movieList = movies.getMovie( );

// The list is live, so we can operate upon it directly
movieList.add(newMovie);
movieList.add(anotherNewMovie);
```

As you can see, the Java List returned is live, so you can simply operate upon it rather than continuing to work with the Movies object. You should also take care with the types that you add to this list, as Java collections are not type-safe; you could just as easily add strings, dates, or other objects that would cause problems later on when converting the objects back to XML.

I also want to advise you against ever using the `property-get-set-prefixes` option. The result is a pair of methods like this:

```
public String title() {
    // implementation
}

public void title(String title) {
    // implementation
}
```

Here, the accessor (for retrieving values) and the mutator (for setting them) have the same method name since the prefixes have been removed. With only the return type and parameters different, this is extremely confusing. Because it doesn't help in any situation, results in confusing code, and requires extra work in the binding schema, I'd urge you to simply stay away from the option.

I realize that I've rushed through most of these details; we'll revisit all of this in detail in the chapter on binding schemas, so don't worry if you're a little dizzy. However, with the basics introduced here, you're ready to get to the actual source code generation and see these options in action for yourself.

Generating Java Source Files

At this point, you've got all of the required components to generate source code from the movie database constraint set. In this section, I detail the actual process of using the command-line tools in JAXB to generate classes. You'll find out how to get set up with the JAXB framework, use the provided scripts, and actually generate classes.

Getting Set Up

The first thing you need to do, if you haven't already, is download the JAXB release. Visit *http://java.sun.com/xml/jaxb* and follow the links to download the reference implementation of JAXB. I also recommend that you download the PDF specification for reference. Once you've got the release (named something like *jaxb-1_0-bin.zip*), you'll want to extract this to a directory on your hard drive. On my Windows machine, I used *c:\dev\javajaxb\jaxb-1.0*, and it's extracted at */dev/javajaxb/jaxb-1.0* on my Mac (running OS X).

You'll want to note the two *jar* files in the *lib/* directory, *jaxb-rt-1.0-ea.jar* and *jaxb-xjc-1.0-ea.jar*. The first is used for JAXB classes at runtime (indicated by the *rt*), and the second contains the classes used in schema compilation. In other words, you'll want the first in your classpath for your applications using generated classes and the second in your classpath when generating those classes.

Additionally, JAXB comes with a script in the *bin/* directory, used for invoking the Java class that starts the schema compiler for class generation. However, at least in the version I've got, this script works only on Unix-based systems. Instructions for invoking the JAXB schema compiler on Windows are available, but they are pretty poor. To help Windows users, Example 3-5 shows a batch file that invokes the schema compiler (and report errors usefully) for Windows systems. I've saved it as *xjc.bat*, also in my *bin/* directory.

Example 3-5. Batch file for class generation using JAXB

```
@echo off

if "%JAVA_HOME%" == "" goto java_home_error
if "%JAXB_HOME%" == "" goto jaxb_home_error

set LOCALCLASSPATH=%JAVA_HOME%\lib\tools.jar;%JAXB_HOME%\lib\jaxb-xjc-1.0-ea.jar

echo Starting JAXB Schema Compiler...

rem The next two lines of text are ONE line in the batch file!!
"%JAVA_HOME%\bin\java.exe" -classpath "%LOCALCLASSPATH%"
    com.sun.tools.xjc.Main %1 %2 %3 %4 %5 %6 %7 %8 %9

goto end

:java_home_error

echo ERROR: JAVA_HOME not found in your environment.
echo Please, set the JAVA_HOME variable in your environment to match the
echo location of the Java Virtual Machine you want to use, like this:
echo    set JAVA_HOME=c:\java\jdk1.3.1

goto end

:jaxb_home_error

echo ERROR: JAXB_HOME not found in your environment.
echo Please, set the JAXB_HOME variable in your environment to match the
echo location of the JAXB installation, like this:
echo    set JAXB_HOME=c:\dev\javajaxb\jaxb-1.0-ea

goto end

:end

set LOCALCLASSPATH=
```

You'll need to set two environment variables before running this batch file: JAVA_HOME (to your JDK installation) and JAXB_HOME (to your JAXB installation). In other words, use the script like this:

```
Microsoft Windows XP [Version 5.1.2526]
(C) Copyright 1985-2001 Microsoft Corp.

C:\Documents and Settings\Brett McLaughlin>cd \dev\javajaxb
```

```
C:\dev\javajaxb>set JAVA_HOME=c:\java\jdk1.3.1

C:\dev\javajaxb>set JAXB_HOME=c:\dev\javajaxb\jaxb-1.0

C:\dev\javajaxb>set PATH=%PATH%;%JAXB_HOME%\bin

C:\dev\javajaxb>xjc
```

I've set the two required environment variables and set my PATH to include the binary directory with the *xjc.bat* script. At this point, you're ready to generate some code.

Supplying Output

Finally, you can get down to the actual fun part. For the sake of these examples, I'm using my Windows system. I'll try to alternate between Windows and the Unix box to give you a sample of both operating systems. Here's my directory layout, so you'll understand how my commands relate to the filesystem I've got set up. Figure 3-2 shows the basic setup, which I'll use for the future chapters as well.

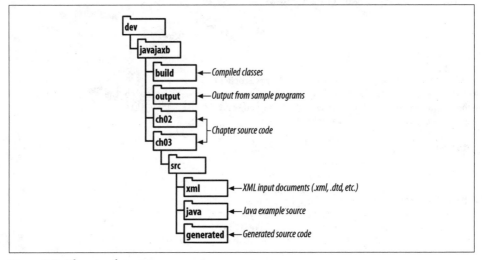

Figure 3-2. Filesystem layout

The movie database DTD is saved as *movies.dtd* in the *xml/* directory, and the *movies.xjs* binding schema is stored in the *bindingSchema/* directory. I've created a *generated/* directory in which to put the source code that JAXB generates. Finally, I'm running the schema compiler from the *javajaxb/ch03/* directory. You can execute the schema compiler script like this:

```
C:\dev\javajaxb\ch03\src>xjc xml/movies.dtd bindingSchema/movies.xjs -d generated
Starting JAXB Schema Compiler...
generated\javajaxb\generated\movies\Actor.java
generated\javajaxb\generated\movies\Cast.java
generated\javajaxb\generated\movies\Movie.java
generated\javajaxb\generated\movies\Movies.java
```

As you can see, the output is almost disappointing after all the work it took to get it going. Each element in the XML document resulted in a single, generated Java source file. Additionally, the package supplied in the binding schema is used to determine the directory in which to place the source files, as well as the package declaration for the source files.

If you change into the *generated/* directory and look at the source files, you'll see that they are pretty complex. In addition to the methods you would expect (getMovie(), setTitle(), etc.), you'll see several other methods, like validate(), marshal(), and unmarshal(). I'll look at these methods more closely in the next two chapters on marshalling and unmarshalling, so don't worry about them now. Before getting to that discussion, though, you need to verify your output and make sure it's ready for use.

Verifying Output

If you're expecting a lot of manual inspection, use of tools, and other fancy inspection instructions, I'm happy to report that you're wrong. To ensure that the generated classes work, all you need to do is ensure that they compile:

```
C:\dev\javajaxb\ch03\src>cd generated

C:\dev\javajaxb>javac -d build ch03\src\generated\javajaxb\generated\*.java
```

They all do, and you can verify that the classes were created with a simple directory listing:

```
C:\dev\javajaxb>dir build\javajaxb\generated\movies
 Volume in drive C has no label.
 Volume Serial Number is 3050-C7C5

 Directory of C:\dev\javajaxb\build\javajaxb\generated\movies

11/07/2001  09:54a    <DIR>          .
11/07/2001  09:54a    <DIR>          ..
11/07/2001  09:54a             5,202 Actor.class
11/07/2001  09:54a               187 Cast$1.class
11/07/2001  09:54a             1,290 Cast$ActorPredicate.class
11/07/2001  09:54a             4,789 Cast.class
11/07/2001  09:54a               190 Movie$1.class
11/07/2001  09:54a             1,256 Movie$ProducerPredicate.class
11/07/2001  09:54a             6,686 Movie.class
11/07/2001  09:54a               193 Movies$1.class
11/07/2001  09:54a             1,300 Movies$MoviePredicate.class
11/07/2001  09:54a             5,580 Movies.class
              10 File(s)         26,673 bytes
               2 Dir(s)  8,806,182,912 bytes free
```

These commands are similar for Unix users. You'll see several classes that resulted, and since things compiled, the JAXB schema compiler obviously did its job. Next, you can add these commands to your classpath and use them in an application.

I realize that you may have expected more; it took quite a few pages to get to the point of schema compilation and then only about a paragraph to make something happen. That's the beauty of data binding; the actual class generation is generally a piece of cake. In the next chapter, I'll show you how to use these classes, converting XML to Java, using the Java objects, and working with the data in an application. For now, just make sure that your classes are all in place, and get ready for some actual action.

Before moving on, you also should take some time to perform this process on your own XML constraints. If you've got DTDs that you are using, or want to use, for data binding, I highly recommend playing around with them. There's simply no substitute for good old trial and error. Once you feel comfortable with the schema compiler and the various global options for binding schemas, you're ready to go on to the next chapter.

CHAPTER 4

Unmarshalling

In this chapter, we move from creating Java source files to creating Java objects. In Chapter 3, you built a framework of objects (compiled source files) that represented your constraints. However, this framework isn't particularly useful on its own. Just as a DTD isn't of much use without XML, generated classes aren't any good without instance data. We take the next logical step in this chapter and work on taking an XML document and generating instance data.

I start out by walking you through the process flow for unmarshalling, which is the technical term for converting an XML document into Java object instances. This will give you the same background as the class generation process flow section did and prepare you to work through the rest of the chapter. From there on, it's all working code. First, I discuss creating instance documents, XML documents that conform to your constraint set. Once you've got your data represented in that format, you're ready to convert the XML into Java; the result is instances of the classes you generated in the last chapter. Finally, I cover how to take this data, in Java format, and use it within your application. You'll want to have your XML editor and Java IDE fired up because there is a lot of code in this chapter; let's get to it.

Process Flow

As in the case of class generation, I want to spend a little time walking through the process flow of unmarshalling XML data into Java objects. This is useful in understanding exactly what happens when you invoke that unmarshal( ) method (or whatever it's called with your framework). Rather than relying on a black box process, you'll be able to know exactly what goes on, troubleshoot oddities in your applications, and maybe even help out the framework programmers with a bug here and there.

1. Construct XML data to unmarshal into Java objects.

2. Convert the XML data into instances of generated Java objects.

3. Use the resultant Java object instances.

Each step is detailed here.

XML Data

First, you need to have some XML data to start with. This probably isn't any great revelation to you, but it's worth taking a look at. You'll need an XML document that matches up with the constraints designed in the class generation process. Additionally, this document must be *valid* with respect to those constraints. Valid means that the structure and data in the document fulfill the data contract set out by your DTD. I talk in detail about how to validate your documents both before and during data binding later on in this chapter.

There's not a lot of complexity in this step, so I won't dwell on it. There are certainly some subtle issues to work through in ensuring that the data in your XML document correctly maps to where it belongs in your Java classes, and I cover that in the more detailed sections of the chapter. For now, though, as long as you've got an XML document and have a set of generated classes from the document's DTD, you're ready to roll.

Java Conversion

The guts of the unmarshalling process is the conversion from XML to Java. This is where the most interesting action takes place in any framework. However, it's also the place where the process itself varies the most between frameworks. While the starting point (an XML document) and ending point (Java object instances) are the same, the "in-between" is not. Still, basic principles that are important to understand are at work, and these basics apply to all frameworks.

First, you'll need to convert your XML data into some form of an input stream (usually an InputStream or Reader in Java parlance). This may seem too simple to be worth mentioning, but it turns out to be an important point. It's a common misconception to think about data binding as a process that takes an XML *file* and converts it to Java instance data. However, it's just as likely that the XML data come from a network stream, email message, or some other medium entirely, as opposed to a static file on a hard drive. This opens up all sorts of possibilities and also allows you to think a bit outside of the box. Consider taking a SOAP message, the response to a questionnaire, or an XML shipping manifest, all from a third party. Instead of having to write SAX or DOM code to deal with this information, data binding allows a simple means of interacting with this business data in a business way—a very handy option to have available.

The actual object that the unmarshal( ) method is invoked on is where variance begins to creep in. For example, using JAXB, generated classes are all concrete; to unmarshal an object, you will have code like this:

```
// Get the input stream for the XML
InputStream inputStream = getXMLInputStream();
```

```
// Unmarshal into an object
Movies moviesObject = Movies.unmarshal(inputStream);

// Operate on the instance data
```

This code would seem to create a problem, though, since Zeus creates interfaces. Because unmarshal( ) must be a static method (you don't have instance data yet, so you can't work on an instance), it must exist only on the implementation. To get around this issue, Zeus generates an additional class, called [top-level-object]Unmarshaller. Since movies is the top-level object in the movie database XML, this would be MoviesUnmarshaller. Invoke the unmarshal( ) method on this object like this:

```
// Get the input stream for the XML
InputStream inputStream = getXMLInputStream( );

// Unmarshal into an object
Movies movieObject = MoviesUnmarshaller.unmarshal(inputStream);

// Operate on instance data
```

You'll see similar variances in other frameworks. In all cases, you should get a Java Object back from this method, which is the top-level Java object instance. Depending on the framework, you may have to cast this object to the expected type, as shown here:

```
// Get the input stream for the XML
InputStream inputStream = getXMLInputStream( );

// Unmarshal into an object
Movies movieObject = (Movies)Unmarshaller.unmarshal(inputStream);

// Operate on instance data
```

Still, while these approaches may vary, the basic result is the same: a Java object instance that you can then use to access the XML data without having to work in XML.

Result Objects

Once you've performed unmarshalling, you're left with a set of result object instances. The returned value from the unmarshalling process, as I already mentioned, is the top-level instance of the unmarshalled XML document. This is going to be an instance of the object that corresponds with the root element of your XML document. It's going to have any references to member objects, as well. Thus, for the movies database shown in the last chapter (Example 3-2), you would end up with an object tree like that shown in Figure 4-1.

Other than understanding this structure, there's not much else to these result objects. In fact, that's what is worth emphasizing here: these result objects are normal, ordinary Java object instances. There aren't any special instructions to use them, gotchas to worry about, or other pitfalls.

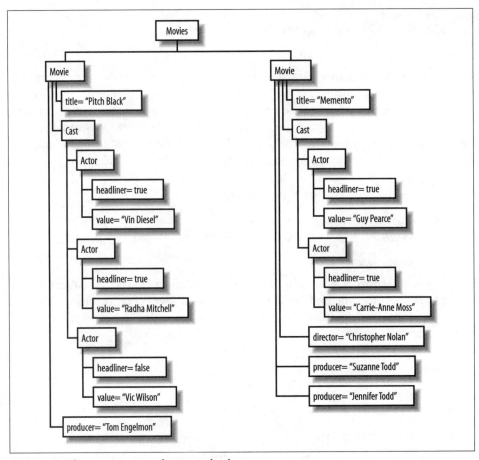

Figure 4-1. Object instance tree for movie database

Use these objects as you would any others, and don't worry about them being data bound. And with that (lack of) admonition, you've got a handle on the unmarshalling process flow. Figure 4-2 illustrates the entire process.

Creating the XML

The first step is to create XML data to be unmarshalled into Java. You'll find that you spend as much time creating XML documents as you do in any other aspect of data binding, as it provides the data for your application. Additionally, it's often easier to open up an editor like notepad or vi than it is to code a program to populate Java objects and then marshal them (although I'll talk about that approach in the next chapter, which focuses on marshalling Java to XML). So let's talk XML.

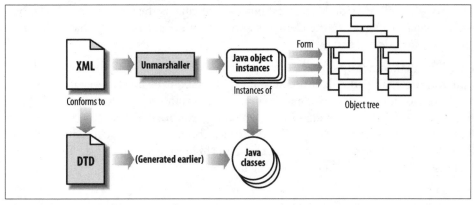

Figure 4-2. Unmarshalling process flow

Authoring an Instance Document

I've spent a lot of time talking about constraint models, setting up your data structure, and other conceptual type ideas. In this section, you get to move a little closer to the practical. Once you've got your constraint model set up (as shown in Chapter 3), you need to model your actual data. In this case, the modeling part of that task is done, and all that is left is filling a document with data. With the emerging XML editor scene, this becomes a piece of cake. For example, Figure 4-3 shows a screenshot of XML Spy, which allows a simple filling of constraints with data; as you can see, this is a trivial task.

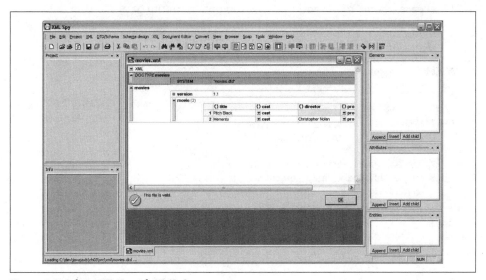

Figure 4-3. Editing XML with XML Spy

Many of you will use simpler editors, but the principle is the same: take a DTD, figure out what data goes in the elements and attributes as defined by that DTD, and create an XML document.

One issue that comes up often is the handling of whitespace. Will the level of indention you use change the data-bound data? What about using tabs versus spaces or single versus double quotes? These issues are important in low-level APIs like SAX because those APIs are intended to give you direct control over the data. However, in higher-level APIs like data binding, these choices become pretty inconsequential. For example, the whitespace between the root and child elements in this document fragment is completely irrelevant when using data binding:

```
<root>
  <child>Here is some text</child>
</root>
```

Because the root element has no actual textual value,* there is no problem with whitespace used in indenting; it's tossed out when the data is unmarshalled. The only issue left is that of whitespace within a textual element, like that shown here:

```
<root>
  <child>  Here is some text with leading and trailing spaces.    </child>
</root>
```

Here, you're going into a vendor-specific paradigm. Some data binding frameworks preserve this space, resulting in the getContent( ) method on the child object returning a value like Here is some text with leading and trailing spaces. Other frameworks trim this text automatically, giving you Here is some text with leading and trailing spaces. Some frameworks give you an option to trim or not to trim this text.

If you know you don't want leading and trailing whitespace (and you usually don't), it's always safe to write code like this:

```
// Get the object
List childElements = root.getChild( );

// Iterate over the children
for (Iterator i = child.iterator( ); i.hasNext( ); ) {
    Child child = (Child)i.next( );

    // Get its value, trimmed
    String childValue = child.getContent( );
    if (childValue != null) {
        childValue = childValue.trim( );
    } else {
        childValue = "";
    }
```

---

* I am assuming that this document's DTD is well written. In other words, the root element has a definition like this: <!ELEMENT root (child)+>. This definition removes the chance that PCDATA slips in and gets turned into a Java object value.

```
      // Do something with the value
  }
```

 Notice that this code compares the returned value from getContent()
to null. While most data binding implementations will not return null
here and instead return an empty string, it never hurts to be careful.
You may save yourself a lot of frustrating debugging by using this
more cautious approach.

Trimming protects you from extra whitespace despite framework variance in
whitespace handling. Other than these minor issues, once an XML document (or documents) is created, you only need to validate them and then unmarshal them into Java.

Validation

I want to address the issue of data validity before getting into the semantics of converting XML to Java. Example 4-1 is a reprint of the XML document representing a
movie database, which I first showed you in Chapter 3.

Example 4-1. Sample movie database

```
<?xml version="1.0" encoding="UTF-8"?>
<!DOCTYPE movies SYSTEM "movies.dtd">

<movies version="1.1">
  <movie>
    <title>Pitch Black</title>
    <cast>
      <actor headliner="true">Vin Diesel</actor>
      <actor headliner="true">Radha Mitchell</actor>
      <actor>Vic Wilson</actor>
    </cast>
    <producer>Tom Engelman</producer>
  </movie>
  <movie>
    <title>Memento</title>
    <cast>
      <actor headliner="true">Guy Pearce</actor>
      <actor headliner="true">Carrie-Anne Moss</actor>
    </cast>
    <director>Christopher Nolan</director>
    <producer>Suzanne Todd</producer>
    <producer>Jennifer Todd</producer>
  </movie>
</movies>
```

This document uses the elements and attributes defined in the *movies.dtd* constraint
set. Because of that, it's a valid document. In other words, it uses only elements and
attributes defined in the DTD and uses the content model specified by that DTD. It
could have been created with XML Spy or by hand; in any case, it fits the constraint
model defined in Chapter 3.

Just taking my word for it isn't such a great idea; you need to be able to verify the document's validity. Many validation frameworks allow you to validate your XML data as it is read in and unmarshalled. However, this adds processing time, which is probably not desired in your application. In many cases, you want some validation at compile time, but not at runtime.

> While I'm all for making applications as fast as humanly possible, removing validation is a delicate issue. If you know that you are going to use an XML document that you have available at compile time, turning off validation makes a lot of sense.
>
> However, data binding is often used to interpret data that is handed off to an application at runtime; for example, consider an application server that reads in deployment information for applications through data binding. In these cases, you probably want to leave validation on at runtime, despite the performance penalty. You can't perform the compile-time validation I refer to in this section, so you need assurance that you're getting valid data and you need to pay whatever price is necessary to get this assurance. Leave validation out, and your data binding may fail with some pretty nasty (and often cryptic!) exceptions.

Because of this, it's helpful to have available a simple utility program that will validate a document against the DTD it specifies through the DOCTYPE declaration, as seen in Example 4-1. To help you in this endeavor, Example 4-2 shows a program that uses JAXP to validate a document.

Example 4-2. Simple validation program

```
package javajaxb.util;

import java.io.File;
import java.io.FileNotFoundException;
import java.io.FileReader;
import java.io.IOException;
import java.io.OutputStream;
import java.io.PrintStream;
import java.io.Reader;

// JAXP classes
import javax.xml.parsers.SAXParserFactory;
import javax.xml.parsers.SAXParser;

// SAX classes
import org.xml.sax.InputSource;
import org.xml.sax.helpers.DefaultHandler;

public class XMLValidator {

    public XMLValidator() {
        // Currently, does nothing
    }
```

Example 4-2. Simple validation program (continued)

```java
    public void validate(Reader reader, OutputStream errorStream) {
        PrintStream printStream = new PrintStream(errorStream);
        try {
            SAXParserFactory factory = SAXParserFactory.newInstance( );
            factory.setValidating(true);

            SAXParser parser = factory.newSAXParser( );
            parser.parse(new InputSource(reader), new DefaultHandler( ));

            // If we got here, no errors occurred
            printStream.print("XML document is valid.\n");
        } catch (Exception e) {
            e.printStackTrace(printStream);
        }
    }

    public static void main(String[] args) {
        if (args.length != 1) {
            System.out.println("Usage: java javajaxb.util.XMLValidator " +
                "[XML filename]");
            return;
        }

        try {
            File xmlFile = new File(args[0]);
            FileReader reader = new FileReader(xmlFile);

            XMLValidator validator = new XMLValidator( );

            // Validate, and write errors to system output stream
            validator.validate(reader, System.out);
        } catch (FileNotFoundException e) {
            System.out.println("Could not locate XML document '" +
                args[0] + "'");
        } catch (IOException e) {
            System.out.println("Error processing XML: " + e.getMessage( ));
            e.printStackTrace( );
        }
    }
}
```

You can compile this class and run it on a document like this:

```
C:\dev\javajaxb\ch04\src\xml>set CLASSPATH=c:\dev\lib\xerces.jar;
    c:\dev\javajaxb\build

C:\dev\javajaxb\ch04\src\xml>java javajaxb.util.XMLValidator movies.xml
XML document is valid.
```

On Unix, it would look like this:

```
bmclaugh@FRODO ~/dev/javajaxb/ch04/src/xml
$ export CLASSPATH=~/dev/lib/xerces.jar:~/dev/javajaxb/build
```

```
bmclaugh@FRODO ~/dev/javajaxb/ch04/src/xml
$ java javajaxb.util.XMLValidator movies.xml
XML Document is valid.
```

As you can see here, I've ensured that the *movies.xml* document is valid with respect to the movies database DTD (*movies.dtd*).

A quick note on using this program: this program assumes that the DOCTYPE reference is relative to the location that the program is run within. Since in this case, the reference is simply movies.dtd, that DTD should be in the directory that the program is run within. You can use a path like *DTDs/movies.dtd* and put the DTD in a subdirectory called *DTDs/*, and it would also work.

You'll also notice that I ensured that a parser (like Xerces) with the JAXP classes, as well as the utility program itself, is included within the classpath. If you forget this step, you'll end up with annoying ClassNotFoundException problems.

Each of your own documents can be run through this simple program to ensure validity at compile time, rather than performing this step repeatedly at runtime. With this step out of the way, you're now ready to convert your XML data into Java object instances.

Converting to Java

Now comes the fun part: turning these XML documents into Java object instances. I'm going to really take this process step by step, even though the steps are awfully simple. The point of this exercise isn't to bore you or fill pages; you need to be able to understand exactly what happens so you can track down problems. As a general rule, the higher level the API, the more that happens without your direct intervention. That means that more can go wrong without the casual user being able to do a thing about it. Since you're not a casual user (at least not after working through this book), you'll want to be able to dig in and figure out what's going on.

XML Input

The first step in unmarshalling is getting access to your XML input. I've already spent a bit of time detailing the process of creating that XML; now you need to get a handle to it through a Java input method. The easiest way to do this is to wrap the XML data in either an InputStream or a Reader, both from the java.io package. When using JAXB, you'll need to limit your input format to InputStreams, as Readers aren't supported (although many other frameworks do support Readers, it is simple enough to convert between the two input formats).

If you know much about Java, there isn't any special method you need to invoke to open a stream; however, you do need to understand what state the stream is in when returned to you after unmarshalling completes. Specifically, you should be aware of whether the stream you supplied to the unmarshalling process is open or closed when returned from the unmarshal( ) method. The answer with respect to the JAXB framework is that the stream is closed. That effectively ends the use of the stream once unmarshalling occurs. Trying to use the stream after unmarshalling results in an exception like this:

```
java.io.IOException: Stream closed
        at java.io.BufferedInputStream.ensureOpen(BufferedInputStream.java:123)
        at java.io.BufferedInputStream.reset(BufferedInputStream.java:371)
        at javajaxb.RereadStreamTest.main(RereadStreamTest.java:84)
```

As a result, you don't expect to continue using the stream, even through buffering or other I/O tricks. That will save you the hassle of writing lots of I/O code, compiling, and then getting errors at runtime and having to rewrite large chunks of your code. If you do need to get access to input data once it has been unmarshalled, you will need to create a new stream for the data and read from that new stream:[*]

```
public static void main(String[] args) {
    try {
        File xmlFile = new File(args[0]);
        FileInputStream inputStream = new FileInputStream(xmlFile);

        // Buffer input
        BufferedInputStream bufferedStream =
            new BufferedInputStream(inputStream);
        bufferedStream.mark(bufferedStream.available( ));

        // Unmarshal
        Movies movies = Movies.unmarshal(bufferedStream);

        FileInputStream newInputStream = new FileInputStream(xmlFile);

        // Read the stream and output (for testing)
        BufferedReader reader = new BufferedReader(
            new InputStreamReader(newInputStream));
        String line = null;
        while ((line = reader.readLine( )) != null) {
            System.out.println(line);
        }
    } catch (Exception e) {
        e.printStackTrace( );
    }
}
```

Other than these somewhat rare issues, if you can write a simple InputStream construction statement, you're ready to turn your XML input into Java output. Be sure to remember that you can use a file, network connection, URL, or any other source for input, and you're all set.

---

[*] This fragment is available as a complete Java source file from the web site, *asch04/src/java/javajaxb/ RereadStreamTest.java*.

Java Output

You should still have the generated source files from the movies database (or your own DTD) from the last chapter. Open the top-level object—the one that corresponds to your root element. If you used the movies DTD, this object is *Movies.java*. Search through the file for the unmarshal( ) methods, which will convert your XML to Java. Here are the signatures for these methods in the Movies object:

```
public static Movies unmarshal(XMLScanner xs, Dispatcher d)
    throws UnmarshalException;

public static Movies unmarshal(XMLScanner xs)
    throws UnmarshalException;

public static Movies unmarshal(InputStream in)
    throws UnmarshalException;

public void unmarshal(Unmarshaller u)
    throws UnmarshalException;
```

Of these four, there's really only one that I care much about—the third one, which I've boldfaced and takes an InputStream as an argument. The reason why the others are less important to common programming is that they involve using specific JAXB constructs; it builds a dependency on JAXB into your application—possibly a specific version of JAXB, which I try to avoid as a general principle. This isn't because JAXB isn't a good framework; I recommend it for any data binding framework, especially when you have the option to use a common input parameter like an InputStream (as discussed in the last section).

The returned object on this method, as well as the other three, is an instance of the Movies class. This shouldn't be surprising, as you want the data in the supplied input stream to be converted into Java object instances, and this is the topmost object of interest. You can then use this object like any other:

```
System.out.println("*** Movie Database ***");

List movies = movies.getMovie( );
for (Iterator i = movies.iterator( ); i.hasNext( ); ) {
    Movie movie = (Movie)i.next( );
    System.out.println("  * " + movie.getTitle( ));
}
```

Here, you'd get a list like this:

```
*** Movie Database ***
  * Pitch Black
  * Memento
```

I'll leave the rest of the discussion of result object use for the next main section, where it can be covered more thoroughly.

Finally, notice that the `unmarshal()` methods are all static. This makes sense, as there is no object instance to operate upon until *after* the method is invoked. Here's how you would turn an XML document into a Java object:

```
try {
    // Get XML input
    File xmlFile = new File("movies.xml");
    FileInputStream inputStream = new FileInputStream(xmlFile);

    // Convert to Java
    Movies movies = Movies.unmarshal(inputStream);
} catch (Exception e) {
    // Handle errors
}
```

I know that probably seems a bit simple after all this talk and detail, but that's really it. What *is* interesting is how the objects are used and where the XML data comes from. I'll take a slight detour into JAXB's inner workings and then address that very topic (JAXB usage) next.

Intermediate Objects

I want to talk briefly about the "in-between" of the JAXB unmarshalling process—in other words, what happens between XML input and Java output. The key classes involved in unraveling this process in JAXB are `javax.xml.bind.Unmarshaller`, `javax.xml.marshal.XMLScanner`, and `javax.xml.bind.Dispatcher`. The `Unmarshaller` class is the centerpiece of the framework and relies heavily on the `XMLScanner` mechanism for parsing. The `Dispatcher` class takes care of mapping XML structures to Java ones. Here's the basic rundown:

First, the JAXB framework presupposes that a full XML parser is not required. The assumption is that because all the XML data is derived from a set of constraints, basic well-formedness rules (like start tags matching end tags) and validity are assured before parsing begins. This hearkens back to my earlier admonition to validate your XML content before using it in a data binding context. Because of these assumptions, an `XMLScanner` instance can operate much like a SAX parser. However, it ignores some basic error checking, as well as XML structures like comments, which are not needed in data-bound classes. Of course, the whole point of this class is to improve the performance issues surrounding parsing data specifically for use in data-bound classes.

Second, JAXB uses a `Dispatcher` to handle name conversion. For every `Dispatcher` instance, there exists a map of XML names and a map of Java class names. The XML names have mappings from XML element names to Java class names (attributes and so forth are not relevant here). The Java class names map from Java classes to user-defined subclasses, in the case that users define their own classes to unmarshal and marshal data into. This class, then, provides several lookup methods, allowing the unmarshalling or marshalling processes to supply an XML element name and get a Java class name (or to supply a Java class name and get a user-defined subclass name).

Finally, the unmarshalling process, through an `Unmarshaller` instance, is accomplished by invoking an `unmarshal()` method on a `Dispatcher` instance. The current `XMLScanner` instance is examined, the current data being parsed is converted to Java (looking up the appropriate name using the `Dispatcher` instance), and the result is one or more Java object instances. Then the scanner continues through the XML input stream and the process repeats. Over and over, XML data is turned into Java data, until the end of the XML input stream is reached. Finally, the root-level object is returned to the invoking program and you get to operate on this object. This is the tale of a JAXB unmarshaller. This process is illustrated more completely in Figure 4-4.

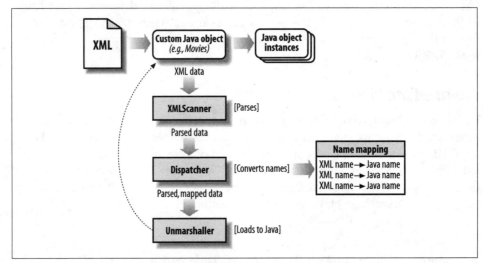

Figure 4-4. The JAXB unmarshalling process in detail

While it's not mandatory that you understand this process, or even know about it, it can help you understand where performance problems creep in (and turn into a bona fide JAXB guru).

Using the Results

So far, the discussions have been technical, but I really haven't shown you how to put it all together. In this section, I will try to show you a couple of interesting uses of data binding and how they can serve as models for your own applications that could benefit from data binding. Hopefully this will finally satisfy your desire to see data binding in practical action.

Business Objects

The most common use of data binding is to turn XML directly into business objects. These objects are given contextual meaning, as in the case of the movie database. The application uses this data as a set of movies, and that use applies meaning to the data. This is quite different from the normal use case for XML (without data binding); in those cases, data has to be extracted and then placed into existing business objects. With data binding, that process is turned into a simple step (the unmarshal( ) method invocation).

As a practical example of this, Example 4-3 introduces the MovieServlet class. This class provides web access, through a GET request, to the data in the current movie database. I won't spend time covering the semantics of servlet code; if you aren't comfortable with servlets, check out Jason Hunter's *Java Servlet Programming* (O'Reilly). In any case, look at the example code, and I'll discuss how the data-bound classes are used.

Example 4-3. The MoviesServlet class

```
package javajaxb;

import java.io.File;
import java.io.FileInputStream;
import java.io.IOException;
import java.io.PrintWriter;
import java.util.Iterator;
import java.util.List;

// Servlet imports
import javax.servlet.ServletConfig;
import javax.servlet.ServletException;
import javax.servlet.http.HttpServlet;
import javax.servlet.http.HttpServletRequest;
import javax.servlet.http.HttpServletResponse;

// Movie database generated classes
import javajaxb.generated.movies.*;

public class MoviesServlet extends HttpServlet {

    /** The Movies database object */
    private Movies movies = null;

    /** Any error that occurred. */
    private String errorMessage = null;

    /** The XML document storing the movie database */
    private static final String MOVIES_XML_DOCUMENT =
        "/dev/javajaxb/ch04/src/xml/movies.xml";

    public void init(ServletConfig config) throws ServletException {
        super.init(config);
```

Example 4-3. The MoviesServlet class (continued)

```java
        // Load the database using JAXB
        try {
            // Load the XML
            File xmlFile = new File(MOVIES_XML_DOCUMENT);
            FileInputStream inputStream = new FileInputStream(xmlFile);

            // Unmarshal
            movies = Movies.unmarshal(inputStream);
        } catch (Exception e) {
            errorMessage = e.getMessage( );
        }
    }

    public void doGet(HttpServletRequest req, HttpServletResponse res)
        throws IOException, ServletException {

        // Handle any error conditions that might have occurred.
        if (movies == null) {
            error(res);
        }

        // Get output stream
        PrintWriter out = res.getWriter( );
        res.setContentType("text/html");

        // Write out movie database
        out.println("<HTML><HEAD><TITLE>Movie Database</TITLE></HEAD>");
        out.println("<BODY>");
        out.println("<H2 ALIGN='center'>Movie Database</H2>");

        List movieList = movies.getMovie( );
        for (Iterator i = movieList.iterator( ); i.hasNext( ); ) {
            Movie movie = (Movie)i.next( );

            // Title
            out.print("<B><FONT SIZE='+1'>");
            out.print(movie.getTitle( ));
            out.println("</FONT></B><BR />");

            // Director
            String director = movie.getDirector( );
            if (director != null) {
                out.print("Director: ");
                out.print(director);
                out.println("<BR />");
            }

            // Producer
            out.println("Producers:<BR /><UL>");
            List producerList = movie.getProducer( );
            for (Iterator j = producerList.iterator( ); j.hasNext( ); ) {
                out.print("<LI>");
```

Example 4-3. The MoviesServlet class (continued)

```
            out.print((String)j.next());
            out.println("</LI>");
        }
        out.println("</UL>");

        // Cast
        out.println("Starring:<BR /><UL>");
        Cast cast = movie.getCast();
        List actorList = cast.getActor();
        for (Iterator j = actorList.iterator(); j.hasNext(); ) {
            Actor actor = (Actor)j.next();
            out.print("<LI>");
            out.print(actor.getContent());
            if (actor.getHeadliner().equalsIgnoreCase("true")) {
                out.print(" (Headliner)");
            }
            out.println("</LI>");
        }
        out.println("</UL>");

        out.println("<HR WIDTH='80%' />");
    }

    out.println("</BODY></HTML>");

    out.close();
    }

    private void error(HttpServletResponse res) throws IOException {
        PrintWriter out = res.getWriter();
        res.setContentType("text/plain");

        out.write(" ************ ERROR OCCURRED **************\n\n");
        out.write("Error: " + errorMessage + "\n");
        out.close();
    }
}
```

Here, a constant is defined with the location of the movies database XML file. You should change this location to match the file location on your system.* In the init() method of the servlet, the movie database is read into memory for all servlet instances. If an error occurs, it is recorded. Of course, this is the single line that makes all the "magic" happen; the XML is converted into business objects, and the top-level Movies instance is stored for later use.

---

* I used an absolute path, which isn't such a great idea, but is simple to understand. In your applications, it's better to put the XML in the same context of your servlet's engine as the servlet itself. This makes security and similar issues much easier to handle.

In the doGet( ) method, this object is used to print out the current movie listings. Simple list manipulation and printing is used here, which is the beauty of data binding. Once the unmarshalling process is complete, only normal Java programming techniques are needed to work with the data. I won't bore you with explanations of the iteration and output code; it's basic Java 101 material. If you load this servlet up in your web browser, you should get output that looks like Figure 4-5.

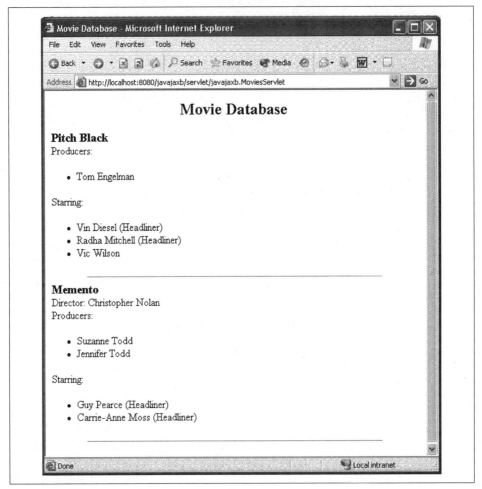

Figure 4-5. The MoviesServlet viewing the database

You will need to make sure that your servlet has access to the generated Java classes from the last chapter (the javajaxb.generated.movies package), as well as the JAXB runtime *jar* file (*jaxb-rt-1.0.jar*). The easiest way to do this, per the servlet 2.3 specification, is to add the classes into your context's *WEB-INF/classes/* directory and the *jar* file into the context's *WEB-INF/lib/* directory. In my setup (Tomcat 4.0.1), I've called my context javajaxb, as you can see in the URL of the web browser in Figure 4-5.

As you can see, there was no data manipulation required to move the data-bound information from XML to business objects; the conversion was direct, which is why data binding is so popular. Business data can be treated as such.

Data Objects

Additionally, it's possible to use data binding to make dealing with data easier. This is most common for configuration data; this information has no business meaning, as did the movie database, but is often easier to work with using data binding than traditional APIs. Building on the movie database servlet, I'd like to show you how to create a standalone Java client to access this information. This client uses XML configuration information, accessed through data binding, to determine how to connect to the servlet and request data.

First, you'll need to set up a DTD and generated classes for this new data set. Example 4-4 is a DTD I saved as *connection.dtd* that will serve as the constraints for this new data. It's a simple DTD that allows a document to specify the host the servlet engine is running on, as well as the URL for the servlet to access.

Example 4-4. The connection DTD

```
<!ELEMENT connection (host, url)>

<!ELEMENT host EMPTY>
<!ATTLIST host
    hostname     CDATA     #REQUIRED
    port         CDATA     #REQUIRED
>

<!ELEMENT url EMPTY>
<!ATTLIST url
        context       CDATA     #REQUIRED
        servletPrefix CDATA     #REQUIRED
        servletName   CDATA     #REQUIRED
>
```

Once you've got Example 4-4 in place, you'll need a simple binding schema to use for the class generation. Example 4-5 is this schema and it specifies only the root element and package for the generated classes.

Example 4-5. The connection binding schema

```
<?xml version="1.0"?>

<xml-java-binding-schema version="1.0-ea">
  <options package="javajaxb.generated.config" />

  <element name="connection" type="class" root="true"/>
</xml-java-binding-schema>
```

With these two documents, you can now generate Java classes and compile those classes:

```
C:\dev\javajaxb\ch04\src>xjc xml\connection.dtd
                            bindingSchema\connection.xjs
                            -d generated
Starting JAXB Schema Compiler...
generated\javajaxb\generated\config\Connection.java
generated\javajaxb\generated\config\Host.java
generated\javajaxb\generated\config\Url.java

C:\dev\javajaxb>javac -d build ch04\src\generated\javajaxb\generated\config\*.java
```

Your directory structure may be different, but the results should be the same: three new compiled classes ready for use in your application programming. Be sure to add these classes to your classpath environment variable, as you'll be using them for the next example.

Next, you need to create an XML instance document with your configuration and connection data in it. Example 4-6 shows my document, which indicates a connection to the servlet running on my local machine, using port 8080 and in the javajaxb context.

Example 4-6. My connection data

```
<?xml version="1.0"?>
<!DOCTYPE connection SYSTEM "connection.dtd">

<connection>
  <host hostname="localhost"
        port="8080" />
  <url context="javajaxb"
       servletPrefix="servlet"
       servletName="javajaxb.MoviesServlet" />
</connection>
```

With all of this in place, you're ready to get started with the client. The complete source for the client is shown in Example 4-7.

Example 4-7. The MovieClient class

```
package javajaxb;

import java.io.BufferedReader;
import java.io.File;
```

Example 4-7. The MovieClient class (continued)

```java
import java.io.FileInputStream;
import java.io.InputStream;
import java.io.InputStreamReader;
import java.net.URL;
import java.util.Properties;

// Connection data binding classes
import javajaxb.generated.config.*;

// Jason Hunter's HttpMessage class
import com.oreilly.servlet.HttpMessage;

public class MovieClient {

    public static void main(String[] args) {
        if (args.length != 1) {
            System.out.println("Usage: java javajaxb.MovieClient " +
                "[XML configuration file]");
            return;
        }

        try {
            File configFile = new File(args[0]);
            FileInputStream inputStream =
                new FileInputStream(configFile);

            // Unmarshal the connection information
            Connection connection = Connection.unmarshal(inputStream);

            // Determine the data needed
            Host host = connection.getHost();
            Url configURL = connection.getUrl();
            String filename = new StringBuffer("/")
                .append(configURL.getContext())
                .append("/")
                .append(configURL.getServletPrefix())
                .append("/")
                .append(configURL.getServletName())
                .toString();

            // Connect to the servlet
            URL url = new URL("http",
                            host.getHostname(),
                            Integer.parseInt(host.getPort()),
                            filename);
            HttpMessage msg = new HttpMessage(url);

            // Indicate we want a listing
            Properties props = new Properties();
            props.put("action", "list");

            // Get response
            InputStream in = msg.sendPostMessage(props);
```

Example 4-7. The MovieClient class (continued)

```
        BufferedReader reader = new BufferedReader(
            new InputStreamReader(in));

        // Output response to screen
        String line = null;
        while ((line = reader.readLine()) != null) {
            System.out.println(line);
        }
    } catch (Exception e) {
        e.printStackTrace();
    }
  }
}
```

In this class, I'm using the com.oreilly.servlet.HttpMessage class introduced in Jason Hunter's servlet book. You can download the class from *http://www.servlets. com/cos/index.html*. Add the entire *jar* file, or just the HttpMessage class, to your classpath and compile the MovieClient source file. This makes sending messages to the movie database servlet very simple. The response from this servlet is obtained as an InputStream, which is buffered and then echoed to the command line.

You'll also see that I'm sending a POST message; a GET message would return an HTML response, which isn't very helpful to a command-line client. That, of course, means you need to go back to the MoviesServlet class and add code that accepts POST requests. This is handy, as I'll revisit this servlet and the doPost() method in the next chapter. For now, the method needs to check the supplied action parameter, and if the value is list, simply return a textual representation of the movies database. Here's the method to add to your servlet:

```
public void doPost(HttpServletRequest req, HttpServletResponse res)
    throws IOException, ServletException {

    // Get action paramater; default is "list"
    String[] actionValues = req.getParameterValues("action");
    String action = null;
    if ((actionValues == null) || (actionValues[0] == null)) {
        action = "list";
    } else {
        action = actionValues[0];
    }

    // Handle different actions
    PrintWriter out = res.getWriter();
    res.setContentType("text/plain");

    /* **** List current movies **** */
    if (action.equalsIgnoreCase("list")) {

        out.write(" ***** Movies Database *****\n\n");
```

```java
            // Print out each movie
            List movieList = movies.getMovie();
            for (Iterator i = movieList.iterator(); i.hasNext(); ) {
                Movie movie = (Movie)i.next();

                // Title
                out.print(" Movie: ");
                out.println(movie.getTitle());

                // Director
                String director = movie.getDirector();
                if (director != null) {
                    out.print("   Director: ");
                    out.println(director);
                    out.println();
                }

                // Producer
                out.println("   Producers:");
                List producerList = movie.getProducer();
                for (Iterator j = producerList.iterator(); j.hasNext(); ) {
                    out.print("     * ");
                    out.print((String)j.next());
                    out.println();
                }
                out.println();

                // Cast
                out.println("   Starring:");
                Cast cast = movie.getCast();
                List actorList = cast.getActor();
                for (Iterator j = actorList.iterator(); j.hasNext(); ) {
                    Actor actor = (Actor)j.next();
                    out.print("     * ");
                    out.print(actor.getContent());
                    if (actor.getHeadliner().equalsIgnoreCase("true")) {
                        out.print(" (Headliner)");
                    }
                    out.println();
                }

                out.println(" ------------------------------ ");
            }
        } else {
            out.write("The action supplied, '");
            out.write(action);
            out.write("', is not currently supported.\n");
        }
        out.close();
    }
```

Once you've added this method, recompile the servlet, restart your servlet engine (if needed), and execute the command-line client. There's nothing complex here; it essentially does what the doGet( ) method does, except in plain text form rather than

HTML. In the next chapter, you'll add handling of various other actions to this method, as marshalling will allow addition, deletion, and editing of the movies in the database. Once you've got the servlet compiled and running, and your `MovieClient` class compiled with the required components on the classpath (JAXB runtime classes, your connection data-bound classes, and the `HttpMessage` class), you can run the client. You should get output like this:

```
bmclaugh@FRODO ~/dev/javajaxb
$ java javajaxb.MovieClient ch04\src\xml\connection.xml
***** Movies Database *****

Movie: Pitch Black
  Producers:
    * Tom Engelman

  Starring:
    * Vin Diesel (Headliner)
    * Radha Mitchell (Headliner)
    * Vic Wilson
-------------------------------
Movie: Memento
  Director: Christopher Nolan

  Producers:
    * Suzanne Todd
    * Jennifer Todd

  Starring:
    * Guy Pearce (Headliner)
    * Carrie-Anne Moss (Headliner)
-------------------------------
```

After working through the examples presented here, you're ready to move on to marshalling. If there's anything in this chapter you aren't clear on, take a moment to get things straight; the pace only picks up from here. You may also want to experiment with your own applications, using unmarshalling in some real-world cases, to get familiar with the process. Once you've got a grip on the conversion from XML to Java, it's time to turn the process around and convert Java back into XML.

CHAPTER 5

Marshalling

Now that you have made it this far, you should start to feel pretty confident. Class generation got you started, and now you have cruised through unmarshalling. Marshalling is almost an exact mirror image of the unmarshalling process, so it should be a real snap at this point. I begin, as has been my custom, by taking the marshalling process flow step by step at a high level. This will give you the perspective needed for the detailed sections in the rest of the chapter.

Once you've got a handle on the basic flow, you'll learn how to take your Java objects and validate the data in them. This ensures that the XML resulting from your Java objects is still legal data for the original data constraints. Then you'll move on to the actual conversion from Java to XML and look at the resultant XML created from this process. Finally, I touch on creating process loops, where data is converted from XML to Java, back to XML, and then back to Java.

Process Flow

By now, you should know the drill here. As in unmarshalling, there are three basic steps in converting a Java object (or set of objects) to XML. They are listed here and then detailed in the following sections:

1. Validate Java objects to ensure data validity.
2. Convert Java data objects into XML documents.
3. Use/store the resultant XML documents.

Java Objects

The first step, validation of Java objects, assumes that you already have Java objects available for conversion to XML. Along with this assumption is another detail that I will discuss in more detail later in this chapter. That detail is whether your Java objects were originally unmarshalled from XML documents.

When using the JAXB framework, only objects that were originally generated by that framework are candidates for marshalling back into XML. This means that your own application objects, even if they are in the JavaBean's format (with accessors and mutators for member variables), are not eligible for conversion to XML. While this might not seem an imposition right now, data binding offers an attractive solution for persisting Java objects to XML. Using XML for persistence doesn't work out with your existing objects (at least when using the current version of JAXB). As a result, you need to make sure you apply the steps in this chapter only to objects originally created using JAXB.

Once your objects are candidates for marshalling, you need to validate the data in these objects. This ensures that the original constraint set used in your XML documents (the DTD, schema, or other format used to generate Java classes) is valid for any new data set on your objects. If an enumeration, for example, is specified and only the values thriller, comedy, and drama are allowed for the genre element, you would not be able to marshal a Java object whose genre member variable was set to the value sci-fi. In the JAXB process flow, generated objects have a validate() method available to them. JAXB requires validation of marshalled objects, or errors can occur at marshal time. You'll see specifics of this in detail in the drill-down section on validation.

Methods of My Own?

I often am asked if it is possible to add in methods to the generated source code. For example, some users might prefer to have a method, toString( ), that returns the XML version of a Java class. Another good example (one of my excellent reviewers came up with this) would be to add a toHtml( ) method that would return an XHTML-compliant version of the class.

The short answer is that it is possible to do this. The slightly longer answer is that you should be very careful when making changes to your generated classes. First, it is very easy to make what appears to be a harmless change and end up breaking the marshalling or unmarshalling process. Thus, if you do want to add functionality, avoid changing existing methods and simply add new ones. For example, the toString( ) method could simply call marshal( ) and pass in a StringWriter. The second thing to watch out for is overwriting your changes in a subsequent class generation. This would cause all of your changes to be lost. A much safer idea is to subclass the generated classes and simply use these subclasses. You avoid both problems mentioned here with little penalty.

XML Conversion

The process of converting a Java object instance into an XML document turns out to be a piece of cake. Like unmarshalling from XML to Java, all of the hard work involved in conversion from Java to XML is taken care of by the JAXB framework.

Specifically, the `marshal()` method is of interest:

```
// Get an output stream for writing
File myOutputXML = new File("output.xml");
movies.marshal(new FileOutputStream(myOutputXML));
```

Like the input stream detailed in Chapter 4, you need only a viable output stream for this process. Also like unmarshalling, you can use a stream wrapping a file (as shown above), an output stream encapsulating a network connection, or anything else you can imagine. Some other forms of the `marshal()` method take JAXB-specific constructs, but you'll rarely need anything other than the basic form that accepts an `OutputStream`.

There is one significant difference between unmarshalling and marshalling, though; the `unmarshal()` method is static, while the `marshal()` method is not. Remember that you used code like this for unmarshalling:

```
// Invoke unmarshal on the ** CLASS **
Movies movies = Movies.unmarshal(someInputStream);
```

For marshalling, the code would look like this:

```
// Invoke marshal on the ** INSTANCE **
movies.marshal(someOutputStream);
```

The former is invoked upon the class, while the latter is invoked upon an *instance* of the class. It's not a difference you are likely to overlook, but just in case, now you know. That said, I want to briefly look at the XML created by the marshalling process.

Resultant XML

There's very little to say about the resulting XML from marshalling, much as there was little to say about the Java objects created during unmarshalling. It's plain-Jane, vanilla XML and can be used as such. Most importantly, it can be fed right back into another unmarshalling process immediately, creating a data binding loop. This is covered in detail later in this chapter, but you should get an idea about how XML from a `marshal()` invocation has no "strings" attached to it. The result is XML that can be used again by data binding; edited in an XML IDE; read in using a lower-level API like SAX, DOM, or JDOM; or passed across the wire in a SOAP message. Once you've gotten that concept down, Figure 5-1 provides a picture to go along with the detailed principles; it represents the marshalling process flow in JAXB.

Validating Java Objects

The first step in getting ready to convert your Java data into its XML equivalent is to ensure that the data in the object instances is appropriate for conversion. You will need to use JAXB's validation, as well as some code of your own, to ensure that errors are handled *before* marshalling occurs. This allows better error handling and also allows you to react, as a programmer, to user error.

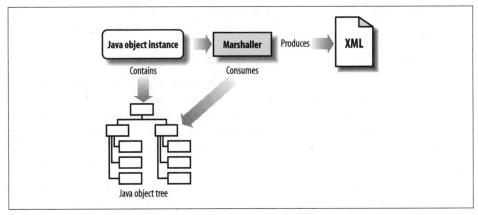

Figure 5-1. The marshalling process flow

Java Validation

The first thing you need to understand about the validation that occurs during JAXB marshalling is that it is by no means perfect. In other words, the validation will catch some problems, but not others. If you don't have a thorough understanding of which errors will be caught and which will not, you will quickly end up with invalid XML from a marshalling process. This invalid XML is often not discovered until much later when that XML is used in some other part of your application.

As a general rule, JAXB will catch only the problems related to missing attributes and elements. The easiest way to see this is through the use of a simple example program. Example 5-1 shows the creation of a new movies database and then the marshalling of that database to XML.

Example 5-1. Errors from missing attributes

```
package javajaxb;

import java.io.File;
import java.io.FileOutputStream;

// Generated Classes
import javajaxb.generated.movies.*;

public class ValidationTest {

    public static void main(String[] args) {
        try {
            // Create a movie database
            Movies movies = new Movies();
            // version attribute NOT set

            // Create a new movie
            Movie movie = new Movie();
```

Example 5-1. Errors from missing attributes (continued)

```
            movie.setTitle("Attack of the Clones");
            movie.setDirector("George Lucas");
            movie.getProducer().add("Rick McCallum");
            movies.getMovie().add(movie);

            // Set cast
            Cast cast = new Cast();
            Actor obiwan = new Actor();
            obiwan.setContent("Ewan McGregor");
            obiwan.setHeadliner("true");
            cast.getActor().add(obiwan);

            Actor anakin = new Actor();
            anakin.setContent("Hayden Christensen");
            anakin.setHeadliner("true");
            cast.getActor().add(anakin);
            movie.setCast(cast);

            // Create output stream
            File file = new File("output.xml");
            FileOutputStream outputStream = new FileOutputStream(file);

            // Marshal back out
            movies.marshal(outputStream);
        } catch (Exception e) {
            e.printStackTrace();
        }
    }
}
```

Note that the version attribute of the movies element was *not* set in this code. If you compile and run this class, you'll get this result:

```
C:\dev\javajaxb>java javajaxb.ValidationTest
javax.xml.bind.ValidationRequiredException
        at javax.xml.bind.Marshaller.marshal(Marshaller.java:91)
        at javax.xml.bind.Marshaller.marshalRoot(Marshaller.java:101)
        at javax.xml.bind.MarshallableRootElement.marshal(
            MarshallableRootElement.java:122)
        at javax.xml.bind.MarshallableRootElement.marshal(
            MarshallableRootElement.java:145)
        at javajaxb.ValidationTest.main(ValidationTest.java:90)
```

JAXB reports that validation *must* occur before marshalling. To fix this problem, add this line of code into the ValidationTest class just before marshalling and recompile:

```
// Validate
movies.validate();

// Create output stream
File file = new File("output.xml");
FileOutputStream outputStream = new FileOutputStream(file);
```

```
// Marshal back out
movies.marshal(outputStream);
```

The result from running this modified class validates the Java class and reports the error:

```
C:\dev\javajaxb>java javajaxb.ValidationTest
javax.xml.bind.MissingAttributeException: version
        at com.oreilly.jaxb.movies.Movies.validateThis(Movies.java:69)
        at javax.xml.bind.Validator.validate(Validator.java:344)
        at javax.xml.bind.Validator.validateRoot(Validator.java:356)
        at javax.xml.bind.ValidatableObject.validate(ValidatableObject.java:124)

        at javajaxb.ValidationTest.main(ValidationTest.java:86)
```

Here, the problem is reported (a missing version attribute). Because the error was reported from the Movies class, you can ascertain that the problem is related to the movies element; the error message, version, tells you what the problem pertains to, and the exception type, MissingAttributeException, explains the cause. While it's not the most elegant solution, it does make determination of the problem possible. There is actually a substantial hierarchy of validation exceptions, and you would be wise to understand how they fit together. To help, Figure 5-2 shows the JAXB validation exception hierarchy.

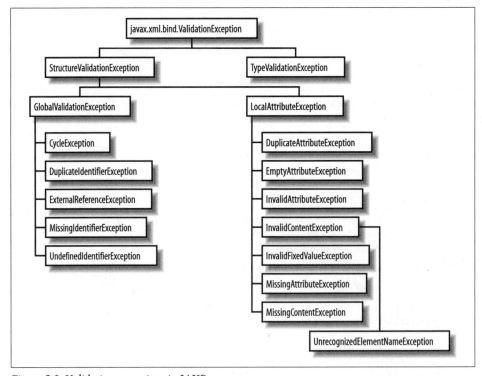

Figure 5-2. Validation exceptions in JAXB

Before you rely on these exceptions too heavily, though, realize that they will not catch all XML errors. Specifically, problems related to the data in elements and attributes are not caught by the validation processes in JAXB.* An example of this is the headliner attribute on the actor element. Here's the definition of that element in the movie database DTD:

```
<!ELEMENT actor (#PCDATA)>
<!ATTLIST actor
          headliner    (true | false)    'false'
    >
```

You can see here that the only allowed values should be true and false. Example 5-2 shows another simple example program that demonstrates reading in a document, changing the value of an actor's headliner attribute to illegalValue, and then marshalling the database back to XML.

Example 5-2. Illegal XML not caught by JAXB

```java
package javajaxb;

import java.io.File;
import java.io.FileInputStream;
import java.io.FileOutputStream;
import java.util.List;

// Generated Classes
import javajaxb.generated.movies.*;

public class ValidationTest2 {

    public static void main(String[] args) {
        if (args.length != 1) {
            System.out.println("Usage: java javajaxb.ValidationTest2 " +
                "[XML movie database filename]");
            return;
        }

        try {
            File xmlFile = new File(args[0]);
            FileInputStream inputStream = new FileInputStream(xmlFile);

            // Read in movies database
            Movies movies = Movies.unmarshal(inputStream);

            /* ******* SETTING INVALID DATA *********** */
            List movieList = movies.getMovie();
            Movie movie = (Movie)movieList.get(0);
```

---

* I expect and hope this behavior to change as JAXB matures. If you receive different results than those shown in the validation section, it's possible that additional validation processes have been added to a version of JAXB released after this book was written.

Example 5-2. Illegal XML not caught by JAXB (continued)

```
        Cast cast = movie.getCast( );
        List actorList = cast.getActor( );
        Actor actor = (Actor)actorList.get(0);
        actor.setHeadliner("illegalValue");

        // Create output stream
        File file = new File("output.xml");
        FileOutputStream outputStream = new FileOutputStream(file);

        // Marshal back out
        movies.marshal(outputStream);
    } catch (Exception e) {
        e.printStackTrace( );
    }
  }
}
```

Unfortunately, you will not get any errors or problems from this code (it compiles and runs fine), although the resultant XML from marshalling is not valid:

```
<?xml version="1.0" encoding="UTF-8"?>

<movies version="1.1">
  <movie>
    <title>Pitch Black</title>
    <cast>
      <actor headliner="illegalValue">Vin Diesel</actor>
      <actor headliner="true">Radha Mitchell</actor>
      <actor>Vic Wilson</actor></cast>
    <producer>Tom Engelman</producer></movie>
  <movie>
    <title>Memento</title>
    <cast>
      <actor headliner="true">Guy Pearce</actor>
      <actor headliner="true">Carrie-Anne Moss</actor></cast>
    <director>Christopher Nolan</director>
    <producer>Suzanne Todd</producer>
    <producer>Jennifer Todd</producer></movie></movies>
```

Obviously, this code never should have made it to XML. That said, every framework is going to have some holes in it; JAXB is no more an exception to this than the other frameworks covered in this book. Your job is to understand where these holes are and be ready to fill them with your own code.

In this particular case, the best way to ensure valid values would be to convert the data type for the headliner attribute into a Boolean. You'll learn how to perform these sorts of type conversions in Chapter 6. In many situations, though, you should treat your generated Java objects much like EJB entity beans: don't expose them to a client directly. In other words, if you wrap these objects in a secondary business layer, you can perform validation in that layer, absolving JAXB of the problems illustrated by ValidationTest2.

For example, consider a class called MovieDatabase that offers methods like this:

```
public class MovieDatabase {

    // Create a new database
    public void addMovie(String title, String director);

    // Add an actor to the cast
    public void addActor(String name, boolean headliner);

    // and so on...
}
```

As you can see, these methods would presumably perform a lot of the grunt work in working with the generated movie objects (like the list manipulation seen in Example 5-2). For example, the constructor for this class might look like this:

```
public MovieDatabase() {
    this.movies = new Movies();
    movies.setVersion("1.0");
}
```

As you can see, the version attribute is taken care of without the user ever worrying about this XML-specific detail. Then the addMovie( ) method might follow:

```
public void addMovie(String title, String director) {
    Movie movie = new Movie();
    movie.setTitle(title);
    movie.setDirector(director);

    // Set an empty cast to avoid NullPointerExceptions later
    movie.setCast(new Cast());

    // Add to the movie database
    this.movies.getMovie().add(movie);
}
```

I won't get into other possible methods, but you get the idea. You'll find that this abstraction layer, and the validation and processing it can contain, will pay off in spades when your XML comes out valid, every time, regardless of your user base.

Finally, you need to always remember to use the validate() method directly before marshalling. For example, look back at Example 5-2: I never invoked validate()! However, the code compiled and ran without the javax.xml.bind. ValidationRequiredException you saw back in Example 5-1. That's because no problems were found; oddly enough, this exception is thrown only when validation problems are found. Without explicitly calling validate(), though, JAXB knows that something is wrong, but cannot handle the problem and report the error. As a result, it's only when problems exist in your Java data objects that a lack of validation shows up. A common result of this gotcha is that you forget to insert the validation invocation, run your application happily for months, and suddenly the program craters because of a validation problem, not with the graceful MissingAttributeException or something similar that is easily understood, but the less-helpful `ValidationRequiredException`. Therefore, always validate and avoid having this sort of problem crop up in production.

Non-JAXB Objects

Although I briefly mentioned it once, it's worth repeating: you cannot marshal non-JAXB-generated classes with JAXB. There's a very simple reason for this: JAXB-generated classes implement some important classes:

```
public class Movies
    extends MarshallableRootElement
    implements RootElement {
```

Without the functionality that the `MarshallableRootElement` (it's `MarshallableElement` in nonroot classes) class provides, validation and marshalling become impossible features to provide.

Be clear that this limitation prevents you from marshalling classes not generated by JAXB; it does *not* prevent you from marshalling JAXB instances that were not unmarshalled. That turns out to be a pretty subtle difference, so let me explain further. If an object class is not generated by JAXB and the xjc schema compiler, it is not a candidate for conversion to XML. However, an object class that is created by JAXB can be converted to XML, regardless of how the instance data is created. That means that you can get instance data into the class by unmarshalling (as seen in Example 5-1) or by using the new keyword and populating the data without unmarshalling (as seen in Example 5-2). Understanding the difference will help avoid confusion when trying to determine if a Java object instance is eligible for marshalling to XML.

Converting to XML

Once you're ready to actually perform the conversion to XML, invoking a `marshal()` method is about as simple as it gets. In this section, I'll continue to use the `MoviesServlet` introduced in Chapter 4 and demonstrate how changes can be made and marshalled back out to XML. This will give you a clear idea of how marshalling works in a realistic way.

Java Input

All that you need for Java input is a set of object instances from JAXB-generated classes. The movie database classes fit the bill, and the instances unmarshalled from the last chapter are perfect candidates. Before bothering to convert these back to XML, though, it makes sense to allow the user to change the values (otherwise, what is the point of marshalling?).

The server

To accommodate modification of the movie database, it is possible to add some new actions to the servlet to complement the "list" action already handled. First, add a few import statements to the class:

```
import java.io.File;
import java.io.FileInputStream;
import java.io.FileOutputStream;
import java.io.IOException;
import java.io.OutputStream;
import java.io.PrintWriter;
import java.util.Iterator;
import java.util.List;

// Servlet imports
import javax.servlet.ServletConfig;
import javax.servlet.ServletException;
import javax.servlet.http.HttpServlet;
import javax.servlet.http.HttpServletRequest;
import javax.servlet.http.HttpServletResponse;

// JAXB imports
import javax.xml.bind.StructureValidationException;

// Movie database generated classes
import javajaxb.generated.movies.*;
```

Each time the servlet marshals to XML, it needs to access the file on the filesystem. In Chapter 4, the xmlFile variable was local to the init() method; however, it should be made a member variable for servlet instances now. You can also modify the init() method to store this member variable for later use:

```
/** The Movies database object */
private Movies movies = null;

/** Any error that occurred. */
private String errorMessage = null;

/** File to unmarshal and marshal to */
private File xmlFile;

public void init(ServletConfig config) throws ServletException {
    super.init(config);

    // Load the database using JAXB
    try {
        // Load the XML
        xmlFile = new File(MOVIES_XML_DOCUMENT);
        FileInputStream inputStream = new FileInputStream(xmlFile);

        // Unmarshal
        movies = Movies.unmarshal(inputStream);
    } catch (Exception e) {
```

```
            errorMessage = e.getMessage( );
        }
    }
```

With this in place, you're now ready to get to the meat of the new work. It's necessary to make a few assumptions about what the client is going to send as arguments; this is possible since you are also writing the client. Table 5-1 summarizes the parameters that are accepted by the servlet.

Table 5-1. Allowed parameters for the MoviesServlet

Argument name	Allowed values
action	list, addMovie, addActor
title	Title of the movie to add
director	Name of movie director
actor	Name of actor to add
headliner	true, false

This will be even more apparent when it's time to make changes to the MovieClient class, discussed later in this section. For now, you need to make changes in the doPost() method that will process these various requests. That involves supporting two new actions, addMovie and addActor. Adding a movie requires a movie title and director, which are easily extracted. Once the modifications are made, marshalling can occur, "saving" the changes to the original XML file. Adding an actor requires specifying which movie to add the actor to, as well as the actor's name and headliner status. This is all basic stuff, so you should look at the modified method and all will be clear:

```
public void doPost(HttpServletRequest req, HttpServletResponse res)
    throws IOException, ServletException {

    // Get action paramater; default is "list"
    String[] actionValues = req.getParameterValues("action");
    String action = null;
    if ((actionValues == null) || (actionValues[0] == null)) {
        action = "list";
    } else {
        action = actionValues[0];
    }

    // Handle different actions
    PrintWriter out = res.getWriter();
    res.setContentType("text/plain");

    /* **** List current movies **** */
    if (action.equalsIgnoreCase("list")) {
        // Handle listing of current movies (see Chapter 4)
    } else if (action.equalsIgnoreCase("addMovie")) {
        out.write(" ***** Adding new movie ***** ");
        String movieTitle = req.getParameterValues("title")[0];
        String movieDirector = req.getParameterValues("director")[0];
```

```java
            Movie movie = new Movie();
            movie.setTitle(movieTitle);
            movie.setDirector(movieDirector);
            movie.setCast(new Cast());
            movies.getMovie().add(movie);

            // Marshal back to XML
            try {
                movies.validate();
                movies.marshal(new FileOutputStream(xmlFile));
            } catch (StructureValidationException e) {
                out.write("Validation error: " + e.getMessage());
                e.printStackTrace(out);
            }
        } else if (action.equalsIgnoreCase("addActor")) {
            out.write(" ***** Adding new actor ***** ");
            String movieName = req.getParameterValues("title")[0];
            String actorName = req.getParameterValues("actor")[0];
            String headliner = req.getParameterValues("headliner")[0];

            List movieList = movies.getMovie();
            for (Iterator i = movieList.iterator(); i.hasNext(); ) {
                Movie movie = (Movie)i.next();
                // See if this is the specified movie
                if (movie.getTitle().equalsIgnoreCase(movieName)) {
                    Cast cast = movie.getCast();
                    Actor actor = new Actor();
                    actor.setContent(actorName);
                    if (headliner.equalsIgnoreCase("true")) {
                        actor.setHeadliner("true");
                    } else {
                        actor.setHeadliner("false");
                    }
                    cast.getActor().add(actor);
                }
            }

            // Marshal back to XML
            try {
                movies.validate();
                movies.marshal(new FileOutputStream(xmlFile));
            } catch (StructureValidationException e) {
                out.write("Validation error: " + e.getMessage());
                e.printStackTrace(out);
            }
        } else {
            out.write("The action supplied, '");
            out.write(action);
            out.write("', is not currently supported.\n");
        }
        out.close();
    }
```

This method allows you to add a new movie to the database and add actors to a specific movie. You can see that the actual task of marshalling back to XML becomes little more than a footnote; the marshal() method and the OutputStream (wrapping the xmlFile variable from the init() method) do all the work for you. This is the reason why data binding has grown so popular: it is incredibly easy to convert between Java and XML. The marshal() method follows validation, and any validation errors are caught and then passed on to the client, indicating what problems occurred.

Of particular note is this snippet of code, when movies are added:

```
Movie movie = new Movie( );
movie.setTitle(movieTitle);
movie.setDirector(movieDirector);
movie.setCast(new Cast( ));
movies.getMovie( ).add(movie);
```

Notice the emphasized line of code. If you do not add an empty Cast instance to the movie being added, the resultant XML would be invalid (a movie element must have a cast element nested within it). This would trigger a validation error, so be sure to add any required structure to your Java representation before marshalling.

One other gotcha is in handling the output streams for marshalling. You might be tempted to change your init() method to something like this:

```
/** Store OutputStream for recurring use */
private OutputStream outputStream;

public void init(ServletConfig config) throws ServletException {
    super.init(config);

    // Load the database using JAXB
    try {
        // Load the XML
        xmlFile = new File(MOVIES_XML_DOCUMENT);
        FileInputStream inputStream = new FileInputStream(xmlFile);

        // Unmarshal
        movies = Movies.unmarshal(inputStream);

        // Create and save output stream for later use
        outputStream = new FileOutputStream(xmlFile);
    } catch (Exception e) {
        errorMessage = e.getMessage( );
    }
}
```

Then, your marshal invocations would look like this:

```
// Marshal back to XML
try {
    movies.validate( );
    // Use member variable, not a new output stream each time
    movies.marshal(outputStream);
```

```
    } catch (StructureValidationException e) {
        out.write("Validation error: " + e.getMessage());
        e.printStackTrace(out);
    }
```

The problem here is that after the first marshalling (whenever a movie is initially added), the JAXB framework would close the output stream provided to the marshal() method. Subsequent marshalling would fail, indicating problems with the outputStream member variable. You should be sure that, each time you marshal your Java objects, you use a new output stream for the process.

The client

All that is left is updating the client to use these new facilities. First, it's worth considering how the tool will be used from the command line. Remember that in the last chapter, the command-line client was run like this:

```
bmclaugh@FRODO ~/dev/javajaxb
$ java javajaxb.MovieClient ch04/src/xml/connection.xml
```

This worked fine for simple listing of the database; however, when it comes to adding a new movie (with a title, director, and actors), it's going to be a pain to keep up with all the arguments and the order in which they are supplied. To help keep track of arguments, you should add the Arguments utility class shown in Example 5-3.

Example 5-3. The Arguments utility class

```
package javajaxb.util;

import java.util.Hashtable;

public class Arguments extends Hashtable {

    public Arguments() {
        super();
    }

    public Arguments(String[] args) {
        super();
        setValues(args);
    }

    public String getValue(String argumentName) {
        return (String)get(argumentName);
    }

    public boolean hasValue(String argumentName) {
        return (get(argumentName) != null);
    }

    public void setValue(String argumentName, String argumentValue) {
        if (argumentName == null) {
```

Example 5-3. The Arguments utility class (continued)

```
                throw new IllegalArgumentException("An Arguments object cannot " +
                    "have a null argument name.");
            }
            put(argumentName, argumentValue);
        }

    public void setValues(String[] args) {
        int equalsPosition = -1;

        for (int i = 0; i < args.length; i++) {
            String arg = args[i];
            equalsPosition = arg.indexOf("=");

            if ( equalsPosition == -1 ) {
                System.err.println("The argument you specified, '"
                    + arg + "' doesn't contain an '='.\n"
                    + "All arguments must be of the form 'foo=bar'.");
                System.exit(1);
            }

            put(arg.substring(0, equalsPosition),
                arg.substring(equalsPosition + 1));
        }
    }
}
```

This class makes it much easier to handle the passed-in arguments and makes the order in which they are supplied irrelevant. You'll see how it is used in the modifications to the MovieClient class. First, add this class to the imports in the client. Then change the format of the input arguments and update the usage instructions. This change allows the user to supply arguments in a format understood by the Arguments utility class. Finally, the supplied arguments need to be converted to parameters for the POST to the movies servlet.

Example 5-4 shows the modified MovieClient class, which has changed substantially from the last chapter.

Example 5-4. The modified MovieClient class

```
package javajaxb;

import java.io.BufferedReader;
import java.io.File;
import java.io.FileInputStream;
import java.io.InputStream;
import java.io.InputStreamReader;
import java.net.URL;
import java.util.Properties;

// Connection data binding classes
import javajaxb.generated.config.*;
```

Example 5-4. The modified MovieClient class (continued)

```java
// Arguments utility class
import javajaxb.util.Arguments;

// Jason Hunter's HttpMessage class
import com.oreilly.servlet.HttpMessage;

public class MovieClient {

    public static void main(String[] args) {
        if (args.length < 2) {
            System.out.println("Usage:\n java javajaxb.MovieClient \n" +
                "    config=[XML configuration file] \n" +
                "    action=[list | addMovie | addActor] \n" +
                "    title=<movie title> \n" +
                "    director=<movie director> \n" +
                "    actor=<actor name> \n" +
                "    headliner=[true | false]");
            return;
        }

        Arguments arguments = new Arguments(args);

        try {
            File configFile = new File(arguments.getValue("config"));
            FileInputStream inputStream =
                new FileInputStream(configFile);

            // Unmarshal the connection information
            Connection connection = Connection.unmarshal(inputStream);

            // Determine the data needed
            Host host = connection.getHost();
            Url configURL = connection.getUrl();
            String filename = new StringBuffer("/")
                .append(configURL.getContext())
                .append("/")
                .append(configURL.getServletPrefix())
                .append("/")
                .append(configURL.getServletName())
                .toString();

            // Connect to the servlet
            URL url = new URL("http",
                              host.getHostname(),
                              Integer.parseInt(host.getPort()),
                              filename);
            HttpMessage msg = new HttpMessage(url);

            // Indicate the action desired
            Properties props = new Properties();
            String action = arguments.getValue("action");
            props.put("action", action);
```

Example 5-4. The modified MovieClient class (continued)

```
            // Add any other required parameters
            if (action.equalsIgnoreCase("addMovie")) {
                String title = arguments.getValue("title");
                String director = arguments.getValue("director");

                props.put("title", title);
                props.put("director", director);
            } else if (action.equalsIgnoreCase("addActor")) {
                String title = arguments.getValue("title");
                String actor = arguments.getValue("actor");
                String headliner = arguments.getValue("headliner");

                props.put("title", title);
                props.put("actor", actor);
                props.put("headliner", headliner);
            }

            // Get response
            InputStream in = msg.sendPostMessage(props);
            BufferedReader reader = new BufferedReader(
                new InputStreamReader(in));

            // Output response to screen
            String line = null;
            while ((line = reader.readLine()) != null) {
                System.out.println(line);
            }
        } catch (Exception e) {
            e.printStackTrace();
        }
    }
}
```

The changes should be self-explanatory at this point. The Arguments class makes argument handling a piece of cake, and the resultant parameters are passed on to the MoviesServlet. Copy your modified servlet into your servlet's context classpath, and restart your servlet engine. You can then use the MovieClient class to add movies and actors and list the modified database:

```
C:\dev\javajaxb>java javajaxb.MovieClient config=ch05\src\xml\connection.xml
action=addMovie title="The Fellowship of the Ring" director="Peter Jackson"
***** Adding new movie *****

C:\dev\javajaxb>java javajaxb.MovieClient config=ch05\src\xml\connection.xml
action=addActor title="The Fellowship of the Ring" actor="Ian McKellan" headliner="
false"
***** Adding new actor *****

C:\dev\javajaxb>java javajaxb.MovieClient config=ch05\src\xml\connection.xml
action=list
***** Movies Database *****
```

```
Movie: Pitch Black
  Producers:
    * Tom Engelman

  Starring:
    * Vin Diesel (Headliner)
    * Radha Mitchell (Headliner)
    * Vic Wilson
--------------------------------
Movie: Memento
  Director: Christopher Nolan

  Producers:
    * Suzanne Todd
    * Jennifer Todd

  Starring:
    * Guy Pearce (Headliner)
    * Carrie-Anne Moss (Headliner)
--------------------------------
Movie: The Fellowship of the Ring
  Director: Peter Jackson

  Producers:

  Starring:
    * Ian McKellan
--------------------------------
```

As you can see, I've added a new movie and actor, which show up when the movie database is listed. This verifies that the live database, stored as Java object instances on the servlet engine, has been modified. You will want to verify that these changes are persisted to the XML database as well, though.

XML Output

The easiest way to perform that verification is to open up the XML file the servlet uses for input and output. Example 5-5 shows how to do this with the two previous modifications.

Example 5-5. Modified XML database

```
<?xml version="1.0" encoding="UTF-8"?>

<movies version="1.1">
  <movie>
    <title>Pitch Black</title>
    <cast>
      <actor headliner="true">Vin Diesel</actor>
      <actor headliner="true">Radha Mitchell</actor>
      <actor>Vic Wilson</actor></cast>
    <producer>Tom Engelman</producer></movie>
```

Example 5-5. Modified XML database (continued)

```
<movie>
  <title>Memento</title>
  <cast>
    <actor headliner="true">Guy Pearce</actor>
    <actor headliner="true">Carrie-Anne Moss</actor></cast>
  <director>Christopher Nolan</director>
  <producer>Suzanne Todd</producer>
  <producer>Jennifer Todd</producer></movie>
<movie>
  <title>The Fellowship of the Ring</title>
  <cast>
    <actor headliner="false">Ian McKellan</actor></cast>
  <director>Peter Jackson</director></movie></movies>
```

Note that the changes made through the movies servlet were marshalled into XML with no problem. More importantly, though, notice some of the subtle changes to the XML document after marshalling. First, some of the spacing has changed; for example, the closing movie and movies tags are not indented as in the original version of the XML. This is an inconsequential change; the two XML documents are *semantically equivalent*. This means that the data is unchanged, although the formatting has changed.

What is a little more important is that the DOCTYPE line in the original XML document has been removed. The JAXB framework does not maintain this information, resulting in marshalled documents dropping the line. I'll spend a little more time on this issue in the next section, but you need to take note of it. The most important thing to understand (at this point) is that marshalling can often introduce some minor changes to the XML documents involved. You should know what these changes are so you do not depend on the presence of something that may disappear after marshalling.

Process Loops

A *process loop* occurs when the output of one process is used as the input for another process. Most often, it refers to using the same process; the output is fed into the process that created the output as input. It's actually easier to visualize this concept than to explain it in words, so let Figure 5-3 be worth a thousand words.

This is particularly relevant to data binding, as you will often marshal Java objects into the same XML file that the instances were unmarshalled from. In fact, that is exactly what has occurred in the case of the MoviesServlet. When the servlet starts up, it reads the XML movie database. When movies or actors are added, marshalling occurs to that same file. The loop occurs when the servlet is restarted and the XML data is read again; in this way, output from marshalling is used as input for unmarshalling. Figure 5-4 fits this into the general diagram in Figure 5-3.

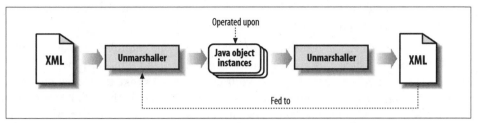

Figure 5-3. Process loops

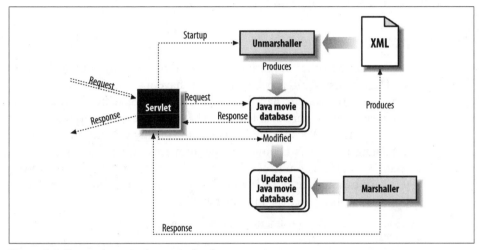

Figure 5-4. Process loops in the movie database

However, process loops have their own set of tricky issues to watch out for. I want to address those issues before going on, as they often come up in data binding situations.

Continuity

The first issue to watch for is continuity. Specifically, a process loop generally involves two discrete data sets, an input and output. However, only one of these data sets is in use at a time in the loops. In data binding, either the XML is used (unmarshalling) or the Java data is used (marshalling). The "exposed" data set should be operated upon.

Problems result, though, when the unexposed data set is visible and edited. For example, if the MoviesServlet starts up, unmarshals the database into Java, and waits for requests, you should operate only on that servlet. If someone were to open up the *movies.xml* file and add a movie, it would marshal its data set back to XML the first time that servlet was used and overwrite the manual edits. The result is a very hard-to-find bug; data scheduling disappears for no apparent reason. Because XML data is generally kept in a normal, static file, it is very difficult to prevent this problem from occurring. One solution (albeit a bit of a hack) is to make the file readable only to the

Windows, though, so isn't foolproof. It also doesn't prevent someone from using root access from causing trouble, either.

The best way to solve the continuity issue is to simply be careful. If you are using an XML file for persistence, don't advertise its existence and educate those who may have access to it. More often than not, your user interfaces (like the servlet created in this and the last chapter) will be easier for clients to interact with. Still, be aware that while XML data is stored in Java object instances, the static representation of that data can be modified, and you will lose that data on the next marshalling from Java back to XML. In this case, forewarned is forearmed.

Equivalence

I have already mentioned that some changes are introduced to your XML documents by the JAXB marshalling process. This can have a lot of impact on process loops, depending on how you are handling the input XML. Specifically, the removal of a DOCTYPE reference can be very problematic. This reference shows up when validation occurs in an XML file. Because JAXB does not explicitly validate an XML document before reading it in, it is common to perform this task manually, especially when the input XML is from an untrusted source (like a network location out of your control). Here's an example code fragment that reads in and validates XML using JAXP, potentially for subsequent use in unmarshalling:

```
SAXParserFactory factory = SAXParserFactory.newInstance();
factory.setValidating(true);
SAXParser parser = factory.newSAXParser();
XMLReader reader = parser.getXMLReader();

// Set handlers up
reader.setContentHandler(myContentHandler);
reader.setErrorHandler(myErrorHandler);
reader.setEntityResolver(myEntityResolver);
reader.parse(inputSource);
```

This will work fine the first time the XML document is read in, as the DOCTYPE reference exists. In other words, no errors will result. However, once the input document has been marshalled back out, the DOCTYPE reference will be omitted. The result is that the second time validation occurs (when the servlet is restarted, for example), you will get errors like this:

```
Element type "movies" must be declared.
Element type "movie" must be declared.
Element type "title" must be declared.
Element type "cast" must be declared.
Element type "actor" must be declared.
Element type "actor" must be declared.
... and so on ...
```

These errors are present because validation is occurring, but no referenced DTD exists to validate against. Obviously, this can be a frustrating bug to track down and even trickier to resolve. There is no clean way to solve this problem; while vendor-specific properties specify a grammar, nothing works across platforms. Your best bet is to bug Sun with your concerns by mailing them problem reports at *jaxb-feedback@java.sun.com*. Expect continued pestering to result in this problem being fixed in upcoming versions of the framework.

At this point, you should feel pretty comfortable with JAXB. Conversion to and from XML, as well as simple class generation, should be under your fingertips. In the next chapter, I'll introduce binding schemas, which will move you beyond the basics to flexible, configurable class generation. This will allow type conversion and the generation of interfaces instead of concrete classes. Make sure you've got your head around the basics so far, and we'll move on to more complex data binding scenarios.

CHAPTER 6

Binding Schemas

Up to this point, I've focused on the simplest cases in data binding. That doesn't necessarily mean that the DTDs and XML documents we've dealt with are simple, but that the transformation and class generation processes are. In other words, the name of an element becomes the name of the Java class, the Java types are defaults (String variables), and no interfaces, inheritance, or other advanced options are used. Discussion of marshalling, unmarshalling, and class generation was easy without these complex options.

Now that you have those basics in place, it's time to introduce these more complex options into the equation. Usually, the simple transformations will not serve your purposes; the names used and the simple string types are not sufficient for effective Java programming. In this chapter, I introduce the numerous options that binding schemas provide and explain how each option affects the classes generated from your DTDs using JAXB.

The format of this chapter differs from what you have seen so far. Many of the first several examples used the generated classes from JAXB. Trying to write even a trivial example for each variation of a binding schema would be impossible and waste a lot of your time. This chapter provides details about binding schema options and showing the resulting changes in your generated classes. I leave it to you to use these modified classes in your programs or in the examples from the previous chapters. Use this chapter as a reference rather than a tutorial, and it will serve you well.

The Basics

Although you looked at binding schemas briefly in Chapter 3, I want to take a moment to look at how binding schemas work before diving into the reference section of this chapter. Like the previous chapters on JAXB, this chapter will help you understand what is going on under the hood of the JAXB schema compiler and should help you make good decisions about which options to use and when.

XML to Java

The most important concept to understand is actually the simplest. A binding schema converts from XML to Java and is a bridge between the two formats. Therefore, you always need to ensure that you have legal XML on the lefthand side of the equation and you have legal Java on the righthand side. Because a binding schema is simply an XML document, no special checks are made to ensure valid Java names. The result is that you are left with that responsibility.

For example, consider the following binding schema fragment, which indicates that an XML element named java-class should be generated as a Java class named Java-Class:

```
<element name="java-class" class="Java-Class" />
```

While this is perfectly legal XML, it will not produce legal Java. A dash (-) is not allowed in Java class names, and although the result is an apparently successful class generation, these classes will not compile. This emphasizes the relationship between a binding schema, Java classes, and Java objects. To understand this concept more clearly, think about the output of the JAXB schema compiler as textual files that conform to the Java source code format. This should clearly indicate that illegal names in Java will not cause problems during class generation, but only during class compilation. Figure 6-1 illustrates this relationship.

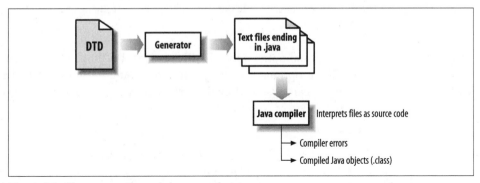

Figure 6-1. Class generation and class compilation

Intermediary Transformations

It's important to understand exactly what happens in the process of converting from XML to Java, particularly with regard to binding schemas. This understanding is important because many frameworks allow you to "hook into" this process and affect the output. This additional control, though, is available only if you know where to step into the process. In reference to binding schemas, some form of transformation must occur to take XML constructs, names, and types and create Java source code with Java names and types.

That said, JAXB does not offer you the chance to interact with this process and it does not create intermediary objects during class generation. That might make this discussion seem a bit of a red herring, but a solid understanding still prepares you to deal with frameworks that allow this interaction, discussed later in the book. The JAXB schema compiler is essentially a tool that blasts out text to a file and constructs a Java source class character by character. It does not create a set of objects from a DTD or create a set of objects for the Java class. This is why issues like illegal Java names are not caught; no source file representation is created that would have these constraints built into the representation.

Structure and Global Options

You've already seen the basic format of a binding schema. The xml-java-binding-schema element is the top-level element, and the version attribute on that element is required. Here's the relevant entry in the binding schema DTD:*

```
<!ELEMENT xml-java-binding-schema
          ( options?, (element | interface | enumeration | conversion)* ) >
<!ATTLIST xml-java-binding-schema
          version CDATA #FIXED "1.0ea" >
```

 The version attribute is the declaration for the 1.0 early-access release of JAXB. As new versions come out, this value is likely to change with those versions.

Although you've seen the global options that JAXB provides, I want to review them briefly in this section. These options are all specified to a binding schema via the options element, which appears just within the top-level xml-java-binding-schema element. The entry for that element is shown here:

```
<!ELEMENT options EMPTY >
<!ATTLIST options
          package                          NMTOKEN        #IMPLIED
          default-reference-collection-type (array | list) "list"
          property-get-set-prefixes        (true | false) "true"
          marshallable                     (true | false) "true"
          unmarshallable                   (true | false) "true" >
```

---

* The actual JAXB binding schema uses parameter entities to refer to some common constructs and thus will not look exactly like the entries shown in this chapter. However, rather than spend time detailing how parameter entities work, I'd rather simplify (as I've done) and stick with information on JAXB. Don't be surprised to see minor differences if you look at the DTD included in a JAXB distribution.

Packaging

Setting the Java package of the generated classes is a matter of using the package attribute on the `options` element:

```
<options package="javajaxb.generated" />
```

You've already seen this in action, so little description is required. Keep in mind that this package applies for all generated classes. There is currently no option for specifying the Java package for only a subset of generated classes. You should also be sure to not add in a trailing period on the package name (like `javajaxb.generated.`), or errors will show up in compilation. Also note that any valid XML character string is allowed here, but Java package names have additional requirements set upon them. For that reason, a value of `$foo` would pass the schema compiler, but cause errors in compilation of the generated classes.

Collection Types

The type of collection to be used is specified through the `default-reference-collection-type` attribute. Valid values for this attribute are `"list"` and `"array"`. The attribute name here is a bit misleading, though; it is not the `ArrayList` or any other Java Collection type that is used when `"array"` is specified, but typed arrays. For a setting like this in a binding schema:

```
<options package="javajaxb.generated"
         default-reference-collection-type="array"
/>
```

you would get methods much like this:

```
public Movie[] getMovie() {
    // Implementation
}

public void setMovie(Movie[] _Movie) {
    // Implementation
}
```

The default for this attribute is the value `"list"`, where true Java Collections are used. Again, you've already seen this in more detail in Chapter 3, so I won't spend additional time on it here.

Properties

The existence of a get and set prefix on property methods is determined by the `property-get-set-prefixes` attribute. The default value for this attribute is `"true"`, but `"false"` is also allowed. In the default case, for an attribute named `"title"`, you would get a `getTitle()` and `setTitle(String title)` method. With this value set to `"false"`, these method names are reduced to `title()` and `title(String title)`. As already discussed, I strongly recommend against using this setting, as it results in extremely confusing code. In any case, here's an example usage:

```
<options package="javajaxb.generated"
         default-reference-collection-type="list"
         property-get-set-prefixes="true"
/>
```

Marshalling and Unmarshalling

The final two options available at a global level are the `marshallable` and `unmarshallable` attributes. Both allow either a `"true"` or `"false"` value, and both default to `"true"`. These attributes determine whether the `marshal()` and `unmarshal()` methods are present on generated classes. While at first these might not seem obvious as useful options, each can address very specific problems.

Leaving off the `marshal()` method results in an object that is, essentially, read-only in terms of its persistent state. It is still possible for an application to invoke methods like `setTitle()` or `addMovie()`; however, the changes made cannot be marshalled back out to XML. If you have configuration data that is immutable in Java or want to protect XML documents from being changed at runtime, you can use this option to achieve that goal:

```
<options package="javajaxb.generated"
         default-reference-collection-type="list"
         property-get-set-prefixes="true"
         marshallable="false"
/>
```

Leaving off the `unmarshal()` method is also useful, although not as much as the `marshallable` option. Leaving off the `unmarshal()` method results in classes that can be populated only through direct object instantiation, using the new keyword. This is appropriate when you want some form of logging or state persisted, but don't ever see a need to read that information. For example, you could use the `marshal()` method to take snapshots of data objects at different times in an application but may leave off unmarshalling abilities since the information is used only for debugging. More often, though, the `"true"` value (the default) is more appropriate:

```
<options package="javajaxb.generated"
         default-reference-collection-type="list"
         property-get-set-prefixes="true"
         marshallable="false"
         unmarshallable="true"
/>
```

When working with both of these attributes, you should remember that the presence (or lack thereof) of methods on a generated class does not affect the memory requirements of that class in a JVM. It shrinks the size of the bytecode, usually in an almost negligible way, but won't improve performance of anything related to it.

Because of this, it's generally a good idea to leave the marshal() and unmarshal() methods in place and make sure they are available if they are ever needed.

Elements and Attributes

The most interesting portion of any binding schema is the instruction set for converting elements and attributes in an XML document to their Java equivalents. This is accomplished through the element and attribute elements in the binding schema and is the subject of the next several sections. I begin by covering elements, then move on to the content allowed within elements, and finally discuss attribute definitions.

Elements

The most common construct you'll use in your binding schemas is the element element (if that's confusing, it's the element named element). This element allows you to specify how conversion occurs from an XML element (like the movie element) to its Java class (currently, the Movie class). The complete DTD declaration for the element element is shown here:

```
<!ELEMENT element ((attribute | constructor | enumeration | conversion)*,
                content?,
        (attribute | constructor | enumeration | conversion)*) >
<!ATTLIST element
        name    ID              #REQUIRED
        type    (value | class) #REQUIRED
        convert NMTOKEN         #IMPLIED
        class   NMTOKEN         #IMPLIED
        root    (true | false)  #IMPLIED >
```

I'll begin by dealing with the allowed attributes and move on to the element's content. The name attribute is simple enough; it indicates the XML name of the element. In the same fashion, the class attribute allows you to specify an alternate name to be used for the Java class. If you wanted to map the movies element in XML to a class named MovieDatabase, you would use the following schema fragment:

```
<element name="movies" type="class" class="MovieDatabase" root="true" />
```

The class attribute is useful, though, only when the type of the element is class. Notice from the DTD declaration that the type attribute can also take on the value class. This is useful for cases in which an element should actually be construed as a simple value, instead of resulting in a complete Java class. For example, look again at the original *movies.xml* file—specifically the actor element. That element has textual content, which is the name of the actor. You might find it annoying to use code like this to add an actor to the database:

```
Actor actor = new Actor();
actor.setContent("Sean Astin");
Cast.getActor().add(actor);
```

Code like this would be much more convenient:

```
Cast.getActor( ).add("Sean Astin");
```

In this case, instead of an Actor object, actors are treated as simple value objects. To accomplish this, you can make the following addition to your binding schema:

```
<element name="actor" type="value" />
```

This will use simple value objects for this element, rather than creating an *Actor. java* source file. However, be careful when using this facility; any attributes on the actor element are ignored and become inaccessible in Java. For example, without the Actor object, you cannot set the status of the headliner attribute. Converting an element to a value object without realizing the full effects of that change can cause some subtle bugs.

The last attribute available is convert. It is useful only when you have specified that the element is a value element rather than a Java class. In this case, the convert attribute can be used to specify a type conversion. Imagine, for example, adding a copyrightYear element as a child of the movie element to indicate the copyright year of the movie being described. You would start by converting this element to a value element, as it would have only the numerical year as its value. Taking this example further, though, you would want to allow only integer values to ensure valid data. The convert attribute would allow you to specify this Java primitive as the type to convert to:

```
<element name="copyrightYear" type="value" convert="int" />
```

In this fashion, you can easily convert value objects to typed value objects, which is one of Java's strengths. I'll talk more about conversions later in the "Attributes" section.

You have already seen the use and purpose of the root attribute, which can have a "true" or "false" value, so I won't spend any additional time on it here. Use it to specify the root element of an XML document and don't worry about it beyond that.

Content Specification

The content of an element is made up of other element references, choices, and sequences, as well as more options for the content structure itself. Here's the complete declaration for the content element:

```
<!ELEMENT content ((element-ref | choice | sequence)*, rest?) >
<!ATTLIST content
        property   NMTOKEN       #IMPLIED
        collection (array | list) #IMPLIED
        supertype  NMTOKEN       #IMPLIED >
```

The elements that can exist nested within the content element are discussed one by one in the next few subsections, and are all very useful; however, I want to treat the attributes on the content element here.

First, I recommend that you avoid using these attributes altogether. The reasoning behind this suggestion is that the attributes and settings that they control affect the content of the parent element as a unit. To get a better idea of this, take a simple DTD element declaration:

```
<!ELEMENT prequel (title, director, releaseYear)>
```

This element has three child elements, all of which make up that element's content. You can treat each of them separately by using element declarations in the binding schema and element-refs in the content of the prequel element. Now consider the following instruction in a binding schema:

```
<element name="prequel" type="class">
  <content property="prequelContent" collection="list" />
</element>
```

The result of this innocuous-looking instruction is that all of the prequel's information is lumped into a single list. Here's the relevant portion of the generated source file:

```
public List getPrequelContent( ) {
    // implementation
}

public void deletePrequelContent( ) {
    // implementation
}

public void emptyPrequelContent( ) {
    // implementation
}
```

What you might not expect is that there are no getTitle(), setDirector(), or getReleaseYear() methods generated in this source file; all references to the element's content in the object are handled through the PrequelContent list. This is the reason why I recommend avoiding using the attributes on the content element; all individuated references to the element's content are lost in favor of a generic, typeless list. Instead, you should use the various constructs outlined below, all of which are elements that can be nested within the content element.

Element references

The standard policy in laying out your binding schema is to make all elements top level (directly under the root element). This makes reading the schema very easy; it also has the subtle effect of making an XML element that may appear in multiple places and at multiple nesting levels available to the whole schema. Schemas that look like this are common:

```
<element name="someParent" type="class">
  <content>
    <element-ref name="child" />
  </content>
</element>
```

```
<element name="someOtherParent" type="class">
  <content>
    <element-ref name="child" />
  </content>
</element>

<element name="child" type="value" convert="float" />
```

However, schemas like the following are hard to work with:

```
<element name="someParent" type="class">
  <content>
    <element name="child" type="value" convert="float" />
  </content>
</element>

<element name="someOtherParent" type="class">
  <content>
    <element name="child" type="value" convert="float" />
  </content>
</element>
```

In the second example, scoping rules require that the nested element appear and be defined twice instead of just once, as in the first example schema fragment. For this reason, the element-ref element, as shown in the first example, allows the content of one element to refer to the definition of another element elsewhere in the schema. In fact, JAXB disallows the second example entirely (as the element element is not allowed as a child of the content element). This is where the element-ref is useful; its definition is shown here:

```
<!ELEMENT element-ref EMPTY >
<!ATTLIST element-ref
        name        NMTOKEN       #REQUIRED
        property    NMTOKEN       #IMPLIED
        collection  (array | list) #IMPLIED >
```

Notice that you are allowed to refer to an element defined globally in the schema, but can still override the property name and collection type. This means that the same XML element, in various locations in an XML document, may be converted to different names and types within Java source files:

```
<!-- Global definition -->
<element name="version" type="value" convert="float" />

<element name="engine" type="class">
  <content>
    <!-- Use the version attribute with default, global settings -->
    <element-ref name="version" />
  </content>
</element>

<element name="descriptor" type="class">
  <content>
    <!-- Use the version attribute, with a different property name -->
```

```
      <element-ref name="version" property="descriptorVersion" />
   </content>
</element>
```

In the default case, the version element (in a made-up example) is, by default, generated as a value called "version". However, the descriptor element indicates that any
XML elements named version nested within its content would be generated into Java
properties named "descriptorVersion". This setting *overrides* the default, global setting. This same principle goes into effect with the collection attribute, allowing local
overriding of the global collection type for a specific element reference.

Choices

The choice element handles cases in which the OR (|) operator is used in a DTD. To
understand this concept, make the following modifications to *movies.dtd*:

```
<!ELEMENT movies (movie+)>
<!ATTLIST movies
          version    CDATA    #REQUIRED
>

<!ELEMENT movie (title, cast, crew, director?, producer*)>

<!ELEMENT cast (actor+)>
<!ELEMENT title (#PCDATA)>
<!ELEMENT director (#PCDATA)>
<!ELEMENT producer (#PCDATA)>

<!ELEMENT actor (#PCDATA)>
<!ATTLIST actor
               headliner    (true | false)    'false'
>

<!ELEMENT crew (filmCrewMember | productionCrewMember | editingCrewMember)*>

<!ELEMENT filmCrewMember (#PCDATA)>
<!ELEMENT productionCrewMember (#PCDATA)>
<!ELEMENT editingCrewMember (#PCDATA)>
```

This DTD adds a new element, crew, which can have several different types of members, each in a different category. If you generate classes from this DTD, the resultant Crew class has only one member variable, a list accessible through getContent().
This is obviously pretty vague, and not appropriate for most applications. The choice
element allows you to indicate the name of that property, as well as the type if you
want to override the global collection type. Take a look at the content model for the
choice element:

```
<!ELEMENT choice EMPTY >
<!ATTLIST choice
          property    NMTOKEN         #REQUIRED
          collection (array | list)  #IMPLIED
          supertype   NMTOKEN         #IMPLIED >
```

You would use this model as shown here:

```
<element name="crew" type="class">
  <content>
    <choice property="members" collection="array" />
  </content>
</element>
```

This definition replaces the vague getList() and related methods with getMembers(), which is obviously much better suited. By specifying "array" as the collection type, you can see the type of object expected by the generated Crew class:

```
public MarshallableObject[] getMembers() {
    // Implementation
}
```

This is a step up from the vague list seen early, as it allows only other MarshallableObjects to be part of the list (such as the generated FilmCrewMember, EditingCrewMember, and ProductionCrewMember classes). If you want to define the type of this array yourself, you can use the supertype attribute, specifying a class name as the value. I won't spend much time on this topic right now, but I will expand on it further when discusing the interface element.

Sequences

The sequence element works exactly like the choice element, except that it handles the AND (,) operator in a DTD. Here is the content model for the element:

```
<!ELEMENT sequence EMPTY >
<!ATTLIST sequence
        property    NMTOKEN           #IMPLIED
        collection (array | list) #IMPLIED
        supertype  NMTOKEN           #IMPLIED >
```

You can make a modification like this to your DTD to see this element in action (I've shown only the modifications):

```
<!ELEMENT movie (title, cast, assistants, crew, director?, producer*)>
```

```
<!ELEMENT assistants (actor, productionCrewMember)+>
```

Here, the assistants element contains pairings of an actor and that actor's assistant, a member of the production crew. You can then make the following DTD modification to customize the property name for this variable:

```
<element name="assistants" type="class">
  <content>
    <sequence property="pairs" />
  </content>
</element>
```

The result is a getPairs() method, which is certainly more descriptive than getContent(), the default generated variable name. You already know how to use the collection attribute, and as with the choice element, I'll come back around to dealing with how to use the supertype attribute.

Rests

The last element allowed as a child of content is rest. Use this element when you have already defined groupings using the sequence and choice elements and want to lump the "rest" of the content into a single property. The content model looks similar to the choice element, in terms of allowed attributes:

```
<!ELEMENT rest EMPTY >
<!ATTLIST rest
        property    NMTOKEN         #REQUIRED
        collection  (array | list)  #IMPLIED
        supertype   NMTOKEN         #IMPLIED >
```

That's actually exactly how attributes defined on the rest element work, just as they did on the content element. Here's a slightly augmented version of the definition of the assistants element to give you a clear picture of how this works:

```
<!ELEMENT assistants ((actor, productionCrewMember)+,
                       (producer, productionCrewMember)*,
                       filmCrewMember*)>
```

Here's the meaning of these changes. First, there are one or more pairings of actors and their assistants (who are members of the production crew). Next, there are additional pairings of the producers and their assistants (also production crew members). Finally, one or more film crew members are listed. These members are (in a rather contrived example) the individuals responsible for managing the assistants. As you can see, this creates a somewhat complex content model. To ensure that all the generated variables maintain meaning, use the following binding schema entry:

```
<element name="assistants" type="class">
  <content>
    <sequence property="actorAssistants" />
    <sequence property="producerAssistants" />
    <rest property="managers" />
  </content>
</element>
```

The first sequence element governs the actor assistants; the second governs the producer assistants; then the rest element comes into play. This element governs the property name for any content remaining in the assistants element—in this case, the names of the managing film crew members. The result is a list of actor-assistant pairings (getActorAssistants()), producer-assistant pairings (getProducerAssistants()), and the rest (getManagers()). As you can see, this allows you to separate complex content models, rather than accepting a vague list of all the content, accessible only through a generic getContent() method. Using the sequence, choice, and rest elements, along with attributes, will result in much better generated classes.

Attributes

The attribute element is used to specify information about how an XML attribute should be handled in class generation. It should always be nested within an element

element, which should make perfect sense; attributes belong to elements in the logical sense. Here's the declaration for the attribute element:

```
<!ELEMENT attribute EMPTY >
<!ATTLIST attribute
          name NMTOKEN #REQUIRED
          convert NMTOKEN #IMPLIED
          property NMTOKEN #IMPLIED
          collection (array | list) #IMPLIED
    >
```

This declaration turns out to be very similar to how elements are handled. The name attribute specified the XML name of the attribute. Its complement on the Java side is the property attribute, which is used as the Java member variable name for the property.

The collection attribute is used if you want to override the global collection option. For example, if you use Java lists globally (the list value in the options element), but want to use typed arrays for this specific property, you could specify the array value for this attribute's collection attribute.

The last attribute, convert, is much more interesting. In the simplest case, you can specify a Java primitive type as the value of this attribute, and JAXB will perform a type conversion, just as it did with elements. For example, if you want the version attribute in your *movies.dtd* file to be a Java float, use float as the value for the convert attribute. However, you may also want to perform conversions to nonprimitive types, like a java.util.Date (a fairly standard task). To accomplish this, you will need to use the conversion element, name that conversion, and refer to that name in the convert attribute. I cover conversions specifically in the next section; for now, realize that this is a reference to a type conversion. Still, you should already understand how this reference can be used to convert character strings to Java primitive types:

```
<element name="movies" type="class" class="MovieDatabase" root="true">
   <attribute name="version"
              property="databaseVersion"
              convert="float" />
</element>
```

Here, the XML attribute version is converted to a Java member variable that will be named databaseVersion. It is also converted to a float data type. You'll get the following methods in your generated source code for the MovieDatabase class:

```
public float getDatabaseVersion( ) {
    // implementation
}

public void setDatabaseVersion(float _DatabaseVersion) {
    // implementation
}
```

You can make the same change to ensure that the `headliner` attribute is always a boolean value:

```
<element name="actor" type="class">
  <attribute name="headliner" convert="boolean" />
</element>
```

And More...

As you saw in the section on elements, several constructs are allowed in binding schemas that are often used throughout a binding schema. These become, essentially, global variables for the schema. They are defined at the top level of a binding schema (nested just within the `xml-java-binding-schema` element). I'll cover each in turn in this section, addressing them in relation to the constructs you've already seen.

You should keep in mind that these are helper constructs. They are useful only when referenced by other elements and attributes. You should take care not to clutter up your binding schemas with enumerations, conversions, and the rest that are not used by other elements and attributes in the schema. This will keep your schemas concise, as well as easily maintainable.

Enumerations

An enumeration is useful when you need to constrain the set of allowed values for an attribute or element. This is particularly useful when your DTD already has these constraints in place; JAXB does not do anything by default to enforce these constraints in your generated classes, but you can add this functionality by using the enumeration element. The definition for this element is shown here:

```
<!ELEMENT enumeration EMPTY >
<!ATTLIST enumeration
        name    CDATA    #REQUIRED
        members NMTOKENS #REQUIRED >
```

To see this definition in action, add the following attribute to the movie definition in your *movies.dtd* constraint set:

```
<!ELEMENT movie (title, cast, assistants, crew, director?, producer*)>
<!ATTLIST movie
        genre  (sci-fi | horror | comedy | drama | mystery | children)  'drama'
>
```

A genre attribute now defines the category that a film falls into. You need to ensure that, on the Java side of the equation, this constraint remains in effect. Without that checking, you can set values on your Java data objects that will, once marshalled back to XML, result in an invalid XML document.

By using the enumeration attribute, you can specify a name for the enumeration and a list of allowed values for that enumeration. Add this declaration to your binding schema:

```
<xml-java-binding-schema version="1.0-ea">
  <options package="javajaxb.generated.movies" />

  <enumeration name="Genre"
               members="sci-fi horror comedy drama mystery children" />

  <!-- Other definitions -->
</xml-java-binding-schema>
```

Although the name of the enumeration is "Genre", that name is not a reference to the genre attribute (these schemas are case-sensitive). Don't be surprised that there is no explicit reference to the attribute; this enumeration is a generic structure and available for use anywhere in the binding schema. This now becomes a named type available for use through the convert attribute on the various constructs already discussed in this chapter. For example, add this reference to the Genre attribute to your binding schema, tying it to your new enumerated value set:

```
<xml-java-binding-schema version="1.0-ea">
  <options package="javajaxb.generated.movies" />

  <enumeration name="Genre"
               members="sci-fi horror comedy drama mystery children" />

  <element name="movies" type="class" class="MovieDatabase" root="true">
    <attribute name="version"
               property="databaseVersion"
               convert="float" />
  </element>

  <element name="movie" type="class">
    <attribute name="genre" convert="Genre" />
  </element>

  <!-- And so on... -->
</xml-java-binding-schema>
```

Now perform class generation. The first thing you should notice is that a new class, Genre, is generated. Here's the basic form of that class (I've omitted some formatting for clarity).

```
package javajaxb.generated.movies;

import javax.xml.bind.IllegalEnumerationValueException;

public final class Genre {

    private String _Genre;
    public final static Genre SCI_FI = new Genre("sci-fi");
    public final static Genre HORROR = new Genre("horror");
```

```java
    public final static Genre COMEDY = new Genre("comedy");
    public final static Genre DRAMA = new Genre("drama");
    public final static Genre MYSTERY = new Genre("mystery");
    public final static Genre CHILDREN = new Genre("children");

    private Genre(String s) {
        this._Genre = s;
    }

    public static Genre parse(String s) {
        if (s.equals("children")) {
            return CHILDREN;
        }
        if (s.equals("comedy")) {
            return COMEDY;
        }
        if (s.equals("drama")) {
            return DRAMA;
        }
        if (s.equals("horror")) {
            return HORROR;
        }
        if (s.equals("mystery")) {
            return MYSTERY;
        }
        if (s.equals("sci-fi")) {
            return SCI_FI;
        }
        throw new IllegalEnumerationValueException(s);
    }

    public String toString() {
        return _Genre;
    }
}
```

This generation makes conversion from a character string (like "sci-fi") to a Genre instance simple, using the static parse() method. You can then look at the source of the modified Movie class, which uses this enumeration for the genre attribute:

```java
public Genre getGenre() {
    // implementation
}

public void setGenre(Genre genre) {
    // implementation
}
```

Simply put, this takes care of any invalid data. You can now write code like this:

```java
someMovie.setGenre(Genre.parse("sci-fi"));
```

Conveniently, you don't have to enclose this code in a try-catch block; the IllegalEnumerationValueException that can be thrown from the Genre.parse() method extends Java's RuntimeException, which means it is unchecked.

Before leaving the enumerations, you should realize that they are equally applicable to elements. If you had declared the genre attribute as an element instead, it might look like this in your movie database DTD:

```
<!ELEMENT movie (title, cast, genre, assistants, crew, director?, producer*)>

<!ELEMENT genre (#PCDATA)>
```

You could then reference the same enumeration in your element definition in the binding schema:

```
<element name="genre" type="value" convert="Genre" />
```

Notice that I'm using the child class as value object; this results in generation of the Movie class with the following methods:

```
public Genre getGenre( ) {
    return _Genre;
}

public void setGenre(Genre _Genre) {
    this._Genre = _Genre;
    if (_Genre == null) {
        invalidate( );
    }
}
```

This code works exactly as the attribute did, where the Genre class generated from the enumeration element defined in your binding schema preserves type-safety. I'd recommend that you make heavy use of the enumeration element, as it adds a tremendous amount of configurability to your generated Java classes.

Conversions

After the section on enumerations, you probably already have a good idea about how conversions work. The definition of the conversion element is shown here:

```
<!ELEMENT conversion EMPTY>
<!ATTLIST conversion
        name  NMTOKEN #REQUIRED
        type  NMTOKEN #IMPLIED
        parse NMTOKEN #IMPLIED
        print NMTOKEN #IMPLIED >
```

You already probably realize that the name attribute is the identifier used by element and attribute elements as the value for their convert attributes. The type attribute should reference an existing Java class. Here's how to define a conversion for Java date types:

```
<xml-java-binding-schema version="1.0-ea">
  <options package="javajaxb.generated.movies" />

  <enumeration name="Genre"
              members="sci-fi horror comedy drama mystery children" />
```

```
<conversion name="Date"
            type="java.util.Date" />

    <!-- Element definitions -->
</xml-java-binding-schema>
```

You can then use this code to require date types in your elements or attributes. First, add a new attribute for the movie element:

```
<!ELEMENT movie (title, cast, assistants, crew, director?, producer*)>
<!ATTLIST movie
          genre  (sci-fi | horror | comedy | drama | mystery | children)  'drama'
          releaseYear  CDATA  #REQUIRED
>
```

Obviously, you want more than just a textual string here; you want a formatted date, and you want to ensure that these same constraints are in place in Java. Thus, you can add a conversion to your binding schema for the releaseYear attribute:

```
<element name="movie" type="class">
  <attribute name="genre" convert="Genre" />
  <attribute name="releaseYear" convert="Date" />
</element>
```

This should be pretty basic to you, so I won't belabor the point. Regenerating classes with this in place will result in two new methods on the Movie class:

```
public Date getReleaseYear( ) {
    // implementation
}

public void setReleaseYear(Date releaseYear) {
    // implementation
}
```

However, the parse and print attributes are a little more interesting. They allow custom formatting of the data, converting to and from the conversion type. Because the XML data type is a simple character string, you need to provide a means to convert from this string to a Java Date (the type supplied in your conversion element) and from that Java format back into a character string. These conversions occur at unmarshalling and marshalling of the Java data objects. Example 6-1 is a utility class that converts from strings to Java dates and back again. It assumes that the incoming string is formatted as "MM/dd/yyyy" or (for example) "05/09/1998". You'll want to enter this class in and compile it, as JAXB will need it momentarily.

Example 6-1. The DateConversion class

```
package javajaxb.util;

import java.text.SimpleDateFormat;
import java.util.Date;

public class DateConversion {
```

Example 6-1. The DateConversion class (continued)

```
    private static SimpleDateFormat df =
        new SimpleDateFormat("MM/dd/yyyy");

    public static Date parseDate(String d) {
        try {
            return df.parse(d);
        } catch (Exception pe) {
            return new Date( );
        }
    }

    public static String printDate(Date d) {
        return df.format(d);
    }
}
```

You next need to let the schema compiler know about these new methods for parsing and printing:

```
<conversion name="Date"
            type="java.util.Date"
            parse="javajaxb.util.DateConversion.parseDate"
            print="javajaxb.util.DateConversion.printDate" />
```

Be sure to include the fully qualified class name, as it will be required for class resolution. While this won't change any code that you'd notice in the generated Movie class, it does add a very important line to the marshalling method:

```
w.attribute("releaseYear", DateConversion.printDate(_ReleaseYear));
```

It also makes a similar addition to the unmarshalling process:

```
_ReleaseYear = DateConversion.parseDate(xs.takeAttributeValue( ));
```

As you can see, the parsing and printing methods become a part of the marshalling and unmarshalling process. This allows JAXB to convert from character data to your custom types.

 You need to ensure that your conversion utility classes, like DateConversion, are in the classpath when compiling your generated classes and running any application that uses them.

Constructors

The constructor element is used to specify nondefault constructors for generated classes. These must appear within an enclosing element element, and that enclosing element must define a class to be generated (the class attribute must be "class", not "value"). The definition of the constructor element is shown here:

```
<!ELEMENT constructor EMPTY >
<!ATTLIST constructor
          properties NMTOKENS #REQUIRED >
```

The only attribute you have to worry about here is the properties attribute, and the value of this attribute should be a list of property names, each separated by a space. To require that the headliner value be supplied in construction of a new Actor class, you would add the following definition to your binding schema:

```
<element name="actor" type="class">
  <constructor properties="headliner" />
  <attribute name="headliner" convert="boolean" />
</element>
```

This definition will generate the following constructor in the *Actor.java* source file:

```
public class Actor ... {

    public Actor(boolean headliner) {
        // implementation
    }
}
```

This is a simple way to add further customization to your classes, increase their ease of use, and require that certain values for a data class be set at object instantiation time.

 Currently, (1.0 early access for the reference implementation and 0.21 for the specification), the constructor element does not work. The preceding behavior is what the specification indicates will happen; changes are certainly possible as this feature is implemented. It also appears that use of the constructor element will remove any default (no-argument) constructors. This is not specifically detailed, but appears to be the behavior that is desired within JAXB.

Interfaces

The last construct I want to discuss is the interface element. Here's it's definition:

```
<!ELEMENT interface EMPTY >
<!ATTLIST interface
          name       NMTOKEN  #REQUIRED
          members    NMTOKENS #REQUIRED
          properties NMTOKENS #IMPLIED >
```

In this case, as with the enumeration element, the name attribute's value becomes the name of a new generated class. The members attribute is used to specify a list of class names; each of these names should correspond to a generated class. Finally, the properties attribute allows a list of properties that should be in common for these generated classes.

To see this in action, add some commonality to the three types of crew members in the movie database DTD:

```
<!ELEMENT filmCrewMember (name, position)>
<!ELEMENT productionCrewMember (name, position)>
<!ELEMENT editingCrewMember (name, position, editingStage)>
```

```
<!ELEMENT name (#PCDATA)>
<!ELEMENT position (#PCDATA)>
<!ELEMENT editingStage (#PCDATA)>
```

Clearly, it does not make sense to have three classes (FilmCrewMember, ProductionCrewMember, and EditingCrewMember), all with a name and a position property, but that don't extend a common base class. Obviously, the editingStage property is unique to the EditingCrewMember class, but the other properties are common. This is a perfect situation for using the interface element. To generate an interface, add this statement to your binding schema:

```
<interface name="Person"
           members="FilmCrewMember ProductionCrewMember EditingCrewMember"
           properties="name position" />
```

The result of this statement is a new generated class, the Person interface, shown in Example 6-2.

Example 6-2. The Person interface

```
package javajaxb.generated.movies;

public interface Person {

    public String getPosition();
    public void setPosition(String position);

    public String getName();
    public void setName(String name);
}
```

This interface is exactly what is desired. However, it doesn't complete the picture. You now need to go back and use the supertype attribute on the various content elements. Remember that the crew element was defined so that its content was referred to simply as a property called members, using the choice element. Here's the original declaration:

```
<element name="crew" type="class">
  <content>
    <choice property="members" collection="array" />
  </content>
</element>
```

This declaration resulted in an array, but the type of the array was simply MarshallableObject; that leaves a lot to be desired in terms of type-safety. By using the supertype attribute in conjunction with the Person interface just defined, you can increase type-safety:

```
<element name="crew" type="class">
  <content>
    <choice property="members"
            collection="array"
            supertype="Person" />
```

```
    </content>
  </element>
```

This change results in two new methods on the generated Crew class:

```
public Person[] getMembers() {
    // implementation
}

public void setMembers(Person[] _Members) {
    // implementation
}
```

 Like the constructor element, use of the supertype attribute appears to be broken in the JAXB 1.0 early-access release. The behavior documented in this section is based on the JAXB specification and should indicate what will happen when bugs in the reference implementation of JAXB are ironed out.

Type safety has been reintroduced and results in a much more Java-centric set of classes. You can make a similar change to the rest element for the content of the assistants element:

```
<element name="assistants" type="class">
  <content>
    <sequence property="actorAssistants" />
    <sequence property="producerAssistants" />
    <rest property="managers"
          collection="array"
          supertype="Person" />
  </content>
</element>
```

The interface element is probably one of the most complex elements offered by JAXB binding schemas and often takes the most time to use efficiently. It is also one of the most important elements available to your binding schemas; it allows the generic lists and arrays generated by JAXB to be type specific and lets you add interfaces to the set of generated classes available to your application.

At this point, you have seen every option JAXB provides in binding schemas, as well as how JAXB generates classes, marshals, and unmarshals. You should feel completely comfortable with the JAXB framework by now and be able to put it to work in the simplest and most complex applications. This chapter closes the proverbial book (at least this one) on JAXB. In the next several chapters, I'll introduce additional data binding frameworks and emphasize how they differ from JAXB. This is not an attempt to steer you away from JAXB, but a presentation of alternate ways to perform the same tasks and provide ways to tackle problems JAXB does not currently solve.

CHAPTER 7

Zeus

Beginning in this chapter and continuing through Chapters 8 and 9, I'll look briefly at three alternate data binding implementations. All three are free, open source packages, and are therefore available for both commercial and private use. I should also make it clear that I do not recommend one implementation over another, nor do I intend to steer you away from using Sun's JAXB reference implementation. However, I firmly believe in choices when it comes to programming, and several are available.

In this first chapter on alternate implementations, I cover the newest data binding implementation, Zeus. Zeus can be found online at *http://zeus.enhydra.org*. Zeus was developed by this author, originally for a short data binding series of article for IBM DeveloperWorks (*http://www.ibm.com/developer*). The Lutris Enhydra Application Server project needed a data binding implementation, though, and this project became a full-fledged effort as open source early in 2001 and moved to SourceForge when Lutris ceased operation. The result is a lightweight data binding implementation that follows the basic guidelines already examined with regard to JAXB, but with some important enhancements.

Process Flow

In this chapter, I begin by examining the process flow of Zeus, particularly how it differs from the JAXB processing you are already familiar with. While the input and output of a Zeus process are largely the same as in JAXB, the internal processes are quite different. Understanding these internals will continue to give you a firm grasp on data binding in general; it may also help you decide which data binding framework you wish to use in your own programming projects.

To remind you of the JAXB processing paths, you may want to review Figures 3-1, 4-2, and 5-1. These figures show the individual processes involved in class generation, unmarshalling, and marshalling. They will be referred to in this section to explain how Zeus behaves in relation to JAXB.

Class Generation

Working with class generation in Zeus is almost identical to JAXB. To begin, you need to construct a constraint model for your document. Currently, Zeus accepts only DTDs, as does JAXB. Zeus allows some additional options, which will be covered later in the chapter. However, these options do not affect the process flow of constraints.

Specifically, Zeus requires a single DTD as input to a class generation process. This DTD is converted to one or more Java classes by the Zeus *binder*. Whereas JAXB used a *schema compiler* (xjc), Zeus uses a binder. You select the binder that matches the constraint type you are using; since Zeus currently supports only DTDs, you would use the DTDBinder. Future versions of Zeus will also support XSDBinder (for XML Schema Definition Language [XML Schemas]), RelaxBinder (for Relax NG schemas), and other popular constraint models. Whichever binder is selected consumes the constraints and parses them.

At this point, Zeus takes a different approach than that used by JAXB. In the JAXB process flow, the schema parser converts the textual constraints directly into Java classes. The result is a *one-pass* class generation process. Zeus, however, uses a *three-pass* architecture for class generation. In the first pass, the binder parses the XML constraints and generates a set of Zeus bindings from these constraints. *Bindings* are Java objects that represent XML constraints. For example, Zeus uses an AtomicProperty, a Container, and a ContainerProperty, to name a few. These bindings are not tied to a particular constraint model; in other words, the bindings created by an XML Schema appear identical to those created from a DTD. This binding creation constitutes the first pass of the class generation process.

In the second pass, these binding objects are processed by a Zeus transformer. *Transformers* in Zeus allow bindings to be filtered, configured, and converted to a modified set of bindings. For example, the use of a binding schema in Zeus would result in a particular type of transformer being used for binding processing. In fact, Zeus has pluggable support for binding schemas from other packages (Castor, JAXB, etc.) through this second-pass layer. The result of the transformer pass is another set of Zeus bindings; this second set represents the bindings ready for conversion to Java classes. You should also realize that multiple transformations can be applied. A binding schema might be used and the resultant bindings then transformed further by programmatic filters. This process allows greater flexibility than in a one-pass architecture.

Finally, in the third pass, Zeus uses a generator to convert the bindings into Java source files. A Zeus *generator* is responsible for converting bindings into static files. Currently, Zeus generates only Java source. However, generators could be written to create other language source files (C, C++, C#, Basic, etc.). More importantly, it is possible to write generators for other constraint languages, like schemas, DTDs, or Relax. The power here is that you can easily read in a constraint set, say a DTD, and convert it to another format, like XML Schema. However, you can reuse the existing parsing behavior of Zeus and would need only to write the static generation process. Thus, the three passes that Zeus makes provide a great deal of flexibility and power not found in other data binding frameworks. Because Zeus is a young project, many of these enhancements are not yet in place; however, as time goes by and others aid in the project's coding, expect to see this pluggability layer fleshed out. Figure 7-1 shows this class generation process in action.

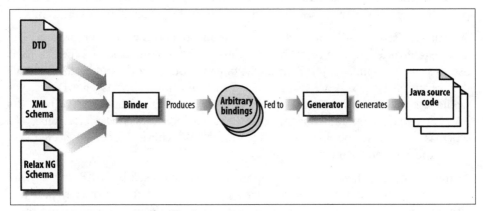

Figure 7-1. The Zeus process flow for class generation

Marshalling and Unmarshalling

Unmarshalling in Zeus is almost identical to unmarshalling in JAXB. Some code-level differences are discussed in later sections (such as working with interfaces versus concrete classes), but the process flow is the same. An XML document is provided to the Zeus unmarshalling engine and converted into a set of Java objects that conform to generated classes.

The same can be said for the marshalling process in Zeus. A set of Java objects can be converted to an XML document through the marshal() method created on generated classes. Specific options available on this method are covered later in this chapter. Still, the premise is identical to that of JAXB and shouldn't cause any confusion when used.

Installation and Setup

With that discussion behind us, you are ready to install and set up Zeus. Go to the Zeus web site at *http://zeus.sourceforge.net*. You can choose to download a Zeus binary distribution or pull the Zeus code directly from CVS. If you are familiar with CVS, you are encouraged to use it; it assures that you obtain the very latest code available.

Once you have grabbed the code, you will need to build the source (unless you downloaded a binary release). Simply use the provided Ant scripts* and run *build.sh* or *build. bat*. You will end up with a *zeus.jar* archive in the *build/* directory, which is what you

---

* Zeus actually comes with an implementation of Ant in *ant.jar*, so you will not need to install Ant separately on your development machine.

get from a binary release download. You should also note that *xerces.jar* and *dtdparser114.jar* are in the *lib/* directories of the Zeus hierarchy. You should include all three of these entries in your classpath, as they are all needed for compile-time tasks:

```
C:\dev\Zeus> set CLASSPATH=c:\dev\Zeus\lib\xerces.jar;
    c:\dev\Zeus\lib\dtdparser114.jar;c:\dev\Zeus\build\zeus.jar
```

Or on Unix:

```
/dev (bmclaugh) $ CLASSPATH=/dev/Zeus/lib/xerces.jar: \
    /dev/Zeus/lib/dtdparser114.jar:/dev/Zeus/build/zeus.jar
```

With your classpath set, you are ready to go.

Class Generation

Now that you have some Zeus ready for use, it is time for a practical discussion. In this section and the rest of the chapter, sample code will be shown to demonstrate how Zeus works. For this example, I'll demonstrate the use of Zeus with a standard web server deployment descriptor, *web.xml*. The sample application will read such a descriptor in and print out various data from the document. This may seem trivial, which is exactly the point.

Reading in a complex XML document and obtaining data from it becomes a trivial task instead of a large coding assignment. Furthermore, you will find it easy to customize the example to display descriptor information in a web application, a Swing GUI, or any other visual style you like.

Justifying Data Binding

There are literally thousands of common applications of data binding. I get a lot of mail asking about suggestions for helping programmers justify the use of data binding. That tells me that developers realize the importance of this technology, but are having a hard time explaining that importance to managers. To help you out, here are a few ideas for getting the point across:

- Junior-level programmers can start coding with XML today, instead of spending weeks learning SAX or DOM.
- It's relatively easy to implement web services using data binding, since SOAP and WSDL are both XML formats that data binding can marshal and unmarshal into.
- You can fire that $400-an-hour SAX consultant and let a full-time employee take over his responsibilities by converting DOM and SAX code to data binding code.
- Exchanging XML with other companies is trivial when using data binding.
- A great new book on data binding explains all of this stuff! (OK, I'm shamelessly plugging myself. It's the only one in the whole book, I promise!)

DTDs

You need to begin with a DTD. The DTD for Sun's *web.xml* descriptor is located online at *http://java.sun.com/j2ee/dtds/web-app_2.2.dtd* and is quite lengthy. I've included just a portion of that DTD in Example 7-1, but you may view it in its entirety online. I've also removed comments from the listing here to preserve space.

Example 7-1. A partial DTD for web.xml descriptors

```
<!ELEMENT web-app (icon?, display-name?, description?, distributable?,
context-param*, servlet*, servlet-mapping*, session-config?,
mime-mapping*, welcome-file-list?, error-page*, taglib*,
resource-ref*, security-constraint*, login-config?, security-role*,
env-entry*, ejb-ref*)>

<!ELEMENT icon (small-icon?, large-icon?)>
<!ELEMENT small-icon (#PCDATA)>
<!ELEMENT large-icon (#PCDATA)>
<!ELEMENT display-name (#PCDATA)>
<!ELEMENT description (#PCDATA)>
<!ELEMENT distributable EMPTY>

<!ELEMENT context-param (param-name, param-value, description?)>
<!ELEMENT param-name (#PCDATA)>
<!ELEMENT param-value (#PCDATA)>

<!ELEMENT servlet (icon?, servlet-name, display-name?, description?,
(servlet-class|jsp-file), init-param*, load-on-startup?, security-role-ref*)>

<!-- And so on... -->
```

Once you have this DTD available (you will need to download it for class generation purposes), you can then generate classes from it. The easiest way to handle class generation is to use the Zeus utility class, `org.enhydra.zeus.util.DTDSourceGenerator`. You can get usage information on this command by running it with no arguments (or refer to Appendix A):

```
C:\dev\Zeus>java org.enhydra.zeus.util.DTDSourceGenerator
Usage: java org.enhydra.zeus.util.DTDSourceGenerator
    -constraints=<constraints filename>
    [-outputDir=<output directory>]
    [-collapseSimpleElements=<true | false>]
    [-ignoreIDAttributes=<true | false>]
    [-javaPackage=<Java package name>]
    [-root=<Root Element Name>]
```

You can check out any options you aren't sure about in Appendix A. For now, simply specify the DTD to generate classes from (-contraints) and the output directory for your classes (-outputDir). Additionally, you should specify a Java package for these generated classes, using the -javaPackage flag.

Use the following command to generate your constraint source code:

```
C:\dev\javajaxb\ch07\src>java org.enhydra.zeus.util.DTDSourceGenerator
    -constraints=xml\web-app_2_2.dtd
    -outputDir=generated
    -javaPackage=javajaxb.generated.web
```

This command is fairly simple and remarkably similar to the invocation of the JAXB class generation tool. You can now verify the classes generated by listing the directory; you should see 128 files. This is a lot of files, though, and perhaps not all are actually necessary. To get an idea of what I'm talking about, open up *web-app_2_2.dtd* and look at the bottom of the file.

I've included a portion here:

```
<!ATTLIST transport-guarantee id ID #IMPLIED>
<!ATTLIST auth-constraint id ID #IMPLIED>
<!ATTLIST role-name id ID #IMPLIED>
<!ATTLIST login-config id ID #IMPLIED>
<!ATTLIST realm-name id ID #IMPLIED>
<!ATTLIST form-login-config id ID #IMPLIED>
<!ATTLIST form-login-page id ID #IMPLIED>
<!ATTLIST form-error-page id ID #IMPLIED>
<!ATTLIST auth-method id ID #IMPLIED>
<!ATTLIST security-role id ID #IMPLIED>
<!ATTLIST security-role-ref id ID #IMPLIED>
<!ATTLIST role-link id ID #IMPLIED>
<!ATTLIST env-entry id ID #IMPLIED>
<!ATTLIST env-entry-name id ID #IMPLIED>
<!ATTLIST env-entry-value id ID #IMPLIED>
<!ATTLIST env-entry-type id ID #IMPLIED>
<!ATTLIST ejb-ref id ID #IMPLIED>
<!ATTLIST ejb-ref-name id ID #IMPLIED>
<!ATTLIST ejb-ref-type id ID #IMPLIED>
<!ATTLIST home id ID #IMPLIED>
<!ATTLIST remote id ID #IMPLIED>
<!ATTLIST ejb-link id ID #IMPLIED>
```

You can see that each element has an ID attribute. However, these attributes really aren't needed by your Java code; they are just used by XML editors and the like. Additionally, you should see that for each of these elements, with only an ID tag, you got an entire source file. For example, you will have a *Remote.java*, *Home.java*, *RoleLink.java*, and so on. These classes have only a textual value.

The result is a lot of clunky Java code like this:

```
String remoteInterface = ejbRef.getRemote().getValue();
String homeInterface = ejbRef.getHome().getValue();
```

This seems to imply that the Home and Remote objects have other properties; however, they don't. They simply have a textual (PCDATA) value and an ID attribute, which really has no meaning to a Java program.

When an element has only textual data, Zeus refers to as a *simple element*. Here's an example of a simple element, called `simple`:

```
<!ELEMENT parent (simple)>

<!ELEMENT simple (#PCDATA)>
<!-- No ATTLIST for this ELEMENT -->
```

By default, simple elements are turned into Java objects, since that is what JAXB does. In this case, you would end up with a class called `Simple`, with only one method: getValue(). However, you can use the `collapseSimpleElements` option in Zeus to collapse this element into its parent. The result would be that no *Simple.java* class would be created. Instead, the `Parent` object (created from the parent of the `simple` element) would have a method called getSimple() on it; that method would return the textual value of the `simple` element. In this way, you would be able to write code like this:

```
String simpleValue = parent.getSimple();
```

Zeus users felt this to be much more intuitive and helpful when programming. Now, let's see how this applies to the web descriptor's DTD. The `home` and `remote` elements appear to be simple as defined in their DTD:

```
<!ELEMENT home (#PCDATA)>
<!ELEMENT remote (#PCDATA)>
```

However, as you recall from the bottom of that file, each element had an `ATTLIST` declaration:

```
<!ATTLIST home id ID #IMPLIED>
<!ATTLIST remote id ID #IMPLIED>
```

This attribute disqualifies them from being simple elements. However, as said several times now, that ID attribute really doesn't help Java programmers and, in this case, prevents them from being able to have these elements collapsed and treated as simple ones. Therefore, the `ignoreIDAttributes` switch can be used. Using this switch instructs Zeus to ignore the ID attribute when determining if an element is simple.

Zeus will not ignore any other attribute. Only the ID attribute is a candidate for this process, as it has no business context or meaning in a data binding application.

Additionally, the `ignoreIDAttributes` flag matters only if you have set `collapseSimpleElements` to true. If that value is false, the `ignoreIDAttributes` flag is completely disregarded.

By collapsing simple elements and ignoring ID attributes, it should be possible to simplify the generated classes. Clear out your generated source files and rerun the command as shown here:

```
C:\dev\javajaxb\ch07\src>java org.enhydra.zeus.util.DTDSourceGenerator
    -constraints=xml\web-app_2_2.dtd
```

```
-outputDir=generated
-javaPackage=javajaxb.generated.web
-collapseSimpleElements=true
-ignoreIDAttributes=true
```

If you create a directory listing on your generated classes, you'll note that the number has gone down from 128 to 48. This is a significant decrease in object overhead and should make your programming tasks much easier! Compile these classes so that they will be ready for use in the next sections.

Future Constraint Models

As already discussed, Zeus will support several other constraint models in future versions. The first model will certainly be XML Schemas, the popular schema model defined by the World Wide Web Consortium (W3C). As discussed in the section on process flow, the architecture of Zeus makes it easier to add support for schemas. The binder, XSDBinder, will need to be written; this binder will parse an XML Schema and convert the schema into a set of Zeus bindings. However, once the Zeus bindings are in place, the mechanics of converting those bindings into Java source files are already complete. The result is that only a small part of schema binding remains to be written. Expect to see support for XML Schema class generation sometime in 2002.

In addition to XML Schema support, there is a lot of buzz surrounding Relax NG, a next-generation schema language. Relax NG is substantially simpler to use and understand than XML Schema and doesn't include support for many of the complex, yet rarely used, features in XML Schema. As a result, it is becoming ideal for use in small- and medium-sized applications or in larger applications in which intercommunication is not as critical. Because of this growing popularity, Zeus plans to support this schema language for data binding to give Relax NG users data binding capabilities. Like the XML Schema binder, a RelaxNGBinder would only need to parse a Relax NG schema and create Zeus bindings. Once that step is done, the existing Zeus framework would take over and handle source code generation. Inclusion of such a binder will most likely depend on a volunteer's work; if you are interested in seeing this functionality, visit *http://zeus.enhydra.org* and sign up for this work today!

Unmarshalling and Marshalling

Once you have a handle on how Zeus deals with class generation, the rest of the package is a piece of cake. Marshalling and unmarshalling in Zeus and JAXB are very similar. I'll walk you quickly through the basics here, although this topic should seem familiar after Chapters 4 and 5.

Unmarshalling

With classes generated and compiled, you need to have an XML descriptor to unmarshal into these Java objects. Example 7-2 is such a descriptor.

Example 7-2. A sample descriptor

```
<?xml version="1.0" encoding="ISO8859_1"?>
<!DOCTYPE web-app PUBLIC '-//Sun Microsystems, Inc.//DTD Web Application 2.2//EN'
                        'http://java.sun.com/j2ee/dtds/web-app_2.2.dtd'>

<web-app>
  <display-name>WebTier</display-name>
  <description>Web Tier DD for the PetStore application</description>
  <servlet>
    <servlet-name>accountcreationsuccess</servlet-name>
    <servlet-class>accountcreationsuccess</servlet-class>
  </servlet>
  <servlet>
    <servlet-name>banner</servlet-name>
    <servlet-class>banner</servlet-class>
  </servlet>
  <servlet>
    <servlet-name>cart</servlet-name>
    <servlet-class>cart</servlet-class>
  </servlet>

  <servlet>
    <servlet-name>webTierEntryPoint</servlet-name>
    <display-name>centralServlet</display-name>
    <description>no description</description>
    <servlet-class>
      com.sun.j2ee.blueprints.petstore.control.web.MainServlet
    </servlet-class>
  </servlet>
  <servlet>
    <servlet-name>populateServlet</servlet-name>
    <display-name>Populate Servlet</display-name>
    <description>no description</description>
    <servlet-class>
      com.sun.j2ee.blueprints.tools.populate.web.PopulateServlet
    </servlet-class>
  </servlet>

  <servlet-mapping>
    <servlet-name>webTierEntryPoint</servlet-name>
    <url-pattern>/control/*</url-pattern>
  </servlet-mapping>
  <servlet-mapping>
    <servlet-name>accountcreationsuccess</servlet-name>
    <url-pattern>/accountcreationsuccess.jsp</url-pattern>
  </servlet-mapping>
  <servlet-mapping>
    <servlet-name>banner</servlet-name>
    <url-pattern>/banner.jsp</url-pattern>
  </servlet-mapping>
  <servlet-mapping>
    <servlet-name>cart</servlet-name>
    <url-pattern>/cart.jsp</url-pattern>
  </servlet-mapping>
```

Example 7-2. A sample descriptor (continued)

```
<session-config>
  <session-timeout>54</session-timeout>
</session-config>
<welcome-file-list>
  <welcome-file>index.html</welcome-file>
</welcome-file-list>
<resource-ref>
  <description>no description</description>
  <res-ref-name>jdbc/EstoreDataSource</res-ref-name>
  <res-type>javax.sql.DataSource</res-type>
  <res-auth>Container</res-auth>
</resource-ref>
<env-entry>
  <description>no description</description>
  <env-entry-name>ejb/catalog/CatalogDAOClass</env-entry-name>
  <env-entry-value>
    com.sun.j2ee.blueprints.shoppingcart.catalog.dao.CatalogDAOImpl
  </env-entry-value>
  <env-entry-type>java.lang.String</env-entry-type>
</env-entry>
<ejb-ref>
  <description>no description</description>
  <ejb-ref-name>ejb/catalog/Catalog</ejb-ref-name>
  <ejb-ref-type>Session</ejb-ref-type>
  <home>
    com.sun.j2ee.blueprints.shoppingcart.catalog.ejb.CatalogHome
  </home>
  <remote>
    com.sun.j2ee.blueprints.shoppingcart.catalog.ejb.Catalog
  </remote>
</ejb-ref>
</web-app>
```

At this point, you need to write code to handle the unmarshalling of this descriptor. Here is where the only real difference between Zeus unmarshalling and JAXB unmarshalling appears. If you take a look at your generated classes, you will notice that Zeus automatically generated both an interface and an implementation class for each XML element. This doesn't affect operation of your objects to any real degree, as Zeus links the two up at marshalling and unmarshalling.

However, this separation of interface from implementation does create some tricky problems in unmarshalling. Recall that since no object yet exists, the unmarshal() method on JAXB was a static method. The same is true for Zeus; since no objects exist yet, there is no object on which to invoke unmarshal(). The result is the need for a static method. However, Java interfaces cannot have static methods or implementations of those static methods in them. Certainly, everyone would agree that this code fragment is awkward and not desirable:

```
WebApp webApp = WebAppImpl.unmarshal(new File("web.xml"));
```

The clean separation of interface from implementation becomes useless when you have to directly refer to the implementation class in code. To get around this chicken-and-egg issue, Zeus generates an additional class for one element in the XML document: the root element. In the case of the *web.xml* descriptor, this would be the web-app element. The normal classes created are *WebApp.java* and *WebAppImpl.java*. However, you will also see *WebAppUnmarshaller.java* in your generated source tree. Example 7-3 shows the content of this class (with most comments and implementation code trimmed out), so you can see what methods are made available by this helper class.

Example 7-3. The WebAppUnmarshaller class

```
package javajaxb.generated.web;

// Global Unmarshaller Import Statements
import java.io.File;
import java.io.FileReader;
import java.io.InputStream;
import java.io.InputStreamReader;
import java.io.IOException;
import java.io.Reader;
import org.xml.sax.EntityResolver;
import org.xml.sax.ErrorHandler;
import org.xml.sax.SAXException;
import org.xml.sax.SAXParseException;

public class WebAppUnmarshaller {
    private static EntityResolver entityResolver;
    private static ErrorHandler errorHandler;

    public static void setEntityResolver(EntityResolver resolver);
    public static void setErrorHandler(ErrorHandler handler);

    public static WebApp unmarshal(File file) throws IOException;
    public static WebApp unmarshal(File file, boolean validate) throws IOException;

    public static WebApp unmarshal(InputStream inputStream) throws IOException;
    public static WebApp unmarshal(InputStream inputStream, boolean validate)
        throws IOException;

    public static WebApp unmarshal(Reader reader) throws IOException;
    public static WebApp unmarshal(Reader reader, boolean validate)
        throws IOException;
}
```

As you can see, this class provides the methods needed to kick off unmarshalling. You can set an error handler (org.xml.sax.ErrorHandler) and entity resolver (org.xml.sax.EntityResolver) to take care of any special processing needs and then kick off unmarshalling with this class. All of the flavors of the unmarshal() method return an instance of the root element class, WebApp, as expected.

With this understanding, you should be able to walk through Example 7-4 easily. This sample class reads in the descriptor provided on the command line and spits out some basic information about the file.

Example 7-4. A simple unmarshalling example with Zeus

```java
package javajaxb;

import java.io.File;
import java.io.IOException;
import java.util.Iterator;

// SAX for ErrorHandler
import org.xml.sax.ErrorHandler;
import org.xml.sax.SAXException;
import org.xml.sax.SAXParseException;

// Generated web.xml classes
import javajaxb.generated.web.*;

public class WebAppDisplayer {

    /** The descriptor to read in */
    private File descriptor;

    /** The object tree read in */
    private WebApp webApp;

    public WebAppDisplayer(File descriptor) {
        this.descriptor = descriptor;
    }

    public void display(boolean validate) throws IOException {
        WebAppUnmarshaller.setErrorHandler(new CommandLineErrorHandler());
        System.out.print("\n\nProcessing ");
        if (validate) {
            System.out.print("and Validating");
        }
        System.out.println("...");
        webApp = WebAppUnmarshaller.unmarshal(descriptor, validate);
        System.out.println("\nProcessed Web XML...");

        // Display some information
        System.out.println("Application Display Name: " + webApp.getDisplayName());
        System.out.println("Application Display Name: " + webApp.getDescription());
        System.out.println("Number of servlets: " +
            webApp.getServletList().size() + "\n");

        // List the servlets
        System.out.println("Listing servlets...");
        for (Iterator i = webApp.getServletList().iterator(); i.hasNext(); ) {
            Servlet servlet = (Servlet)i.next();
            System.out.println(" * Servlet name: " + servlet.getServletName());
```

Example 7-4. A simple unmarshalling example with Zeus (continued)

```
                System.out.println(" * Servlet class: " +
                    servlet.getServletClass( ) + "\n");
        }
    }

    public static void main(String[] args) {
        try {
            if (args.length != 1) {
                System.out.println("Usage: java javajaxb.WebAppDisplayer " +
                    "[web.xml filename]");
                return;
            }

            WebAppDisplayer displayer = new WebAppDisplayer(new File(args[0]));
            displayer.display(true);
        } catch (Exception e) {
            e.printStackTrace( );
        }
    }
}

class CommandLineErrorHandler implements ErrorHandler {

    public void warning(SAXParseException e) throws SAXException {
        // No action... warnings are OK
    }

    public void error(SAXParseException e) throws SAXException {
        System.out.println("Error occurred: " + e.getMessage( ));
        throw e;
    }

    public void fatalError(SAXParseException e) throws SAXException {
        System.out.println("Fatal error occurred: " + e.getMessage( ));
        throw e;
    }
}
```

As mentioned at the beginning of this chapter, the example here is fairly trivial. It unmarshals an XML document into Java and then prints some of the information obtained from the file. However, you should be able to clearly see how unmarshalling, error handling, and validation are dealt with, enabling you to use Zeus in your own programs. Rather than spend a lot of time on business logic that you probably won't use for your own specific tasks, I've kept this information basic and concise.

Marshalling

The process of marshalling in Zeus is even simpler and akin to that in JAXB. The generated classes (and interfaces) all have variations of the marshal() method available for use:

```
public void marshal(File file) throws IOException;
public void marshal(OutputStream outputStream) throws IOException;
public void marshal(Writer writer) throws IOException;
```

This provides analogs to the three unmarshalling methods, allowing the use of a Java File, OutputStream, or Writer. Additionally, Zeus provides two methods that go hand in hand with marshalling:

```
public void setDocType(String name, String publicID, String systemID);

public void setOutputEncoding(String outputEncoding);
```

Both methods affect the output document from a marshalling process. The encoding is added to the XML declaration and the DOCTYPE is added when that method is used.

As in the case of unmarshalling, I won't spend a lot of time discussing information you already know. With that principle in mind, here's a modified version of the WebAppDisplayer sample program, which makes simple changes to the XML deployment descriptor and then writes it back out:

```
// Existing package and import declarations

public class WebAppDisplayer {

    /** The descriptor to read in */
    private File descriptor;

    /** The output file to write to */
    private File outputFile;

    /** The object tree read in */
    private WebApp webApp;

    public WebAppDisplayer(File descriptor, File outputFile) {
        this.descriptor = descriptor;
        this.outputFile = outputFile;
    }

    // Other existing method implementations

    public void modify() throws IOException {
        // Change the encoding
        webApp.setOutputEncoding("ISO-8859-1");

        // Change the DTD to a local version
        webApp.setDocType("web-app", null, "dtds/sun/web-app_2_2.dtd");
```

```
        // Modify the display name
        webApp.setDisplayName(webApp.getDisplayName() +
            " [Modified by WebAppDisplayer]");

        // Add a new servlet
        Servlet servlet = new ServletImpl();
        servlet.setServletName("WelcomeServlet");
        servlet.setServletClass("javajaxb.servlet.WelcomeServlet");
        webApp.addServlet(servlet);

        // marshal
        webApp.marshal(outputFile);
    }

    public static void main(String[] args) {
        try {
            if (args.length != 2) {
                System.out.println("Usage: java javajaxb.WebAppDisplayer " +
                    "[web.xml filename] [output.xml filename]");
                return;
            }

            WebAppDisplayer displayer =
                new WebAppDisplayer(new File(args[0]), new File(args[1]));
            displayer.display(true);
            displayer.modify();
        } catch (Exception e) {
            e.printStackTrace();
        }
    }
}
```

Running this program will produce the following XML document (I've cut out the unchanged portions):

```
<?xml version="1.0" encoding="ISO-8859-1"?>

<!DOCTYPE web-app SYSTEM "dtds/sun/web-app_2_2.dtd">
<web-app>
  <display-name>WebTier [Modified by WebAppDisplayer]</display-name>
  <description>Web Tier DD for the PetStore application</description>

  <!-- Existing servlets -->
  <servlet>
    <servlet-name>WelcomeServlet</servlet-name>
    <servlet-class>javajaxb.servlet.WelcomeServlet</servlet-class>
  </servlet>

  <!-- Other normal declarations -->
</web-app>
```

As you can see, there's nothing too complex to worry about here. With this basic understanding of class generation, unmarshalling, and marshalling, you've got everything you need to understand the basics of Zeus.

Additional Features

In addition to the unique three-pass architecture, Zeus offers several features beyond the standardized data binding functionality defined by JAXB. If these features are particularly attractive to you, you may want to consider using Zeus in your own applications so that you can take advantage of them.

Self-Containment

One of the more powerful features of Zeus is the self-containment that its classes have. If you recall from the earlier chapters, JAXB-generated classes must be added to the application classpath once compiled. Additionally, the JAXB classes themselves were required for operation. Many of the mechanics of marshalling and unmarshalling, as well as exception handling, are in the JAXB *jar* file, and these must be available for use at runtime. However, this builds in a version dependency on JAXB and can sometimes result in two different applications, using different versions of JAXB, being unable to communicate. Marshaled objects in one version may not be unmarshallable in another.

As a result, Zeus removes any runtime dependency on the *zeus.jar* archive. When Zeus classes are generated, they include all necessary facilities for marshalling and unmarshalling, including exceptions. The only external requirement that these classes have is a SAX-compliant parser for XML processing. This can be Xerces, Crimson, or any commercial parser; in fact, you can use one parser for class generation and another for runtime marshalling and unmarshalling.

The generated classes, then, are self-contained. At runtime, you need only the classes themselves and your SAX parser in the classpath. The result is that any version dependencies are removed; the classes themselves contain all of the needed SAX logic to handle unmarshalling, as well as code to write themselves out. For a better idea of how this works, look at some of your generated classes. Here is the header (without comments) of the *WebAppImpl.java* implementation class:

```
package javajaxb.generated.web;

public class WebAppImpl extends DefaultHandler
                    implements Unmarshallable, LexicalHandler, WebApp {

    // Class code
}
```

Obviously, this class implements the WebApp interface, which is generated by Zeus. It also implements another generated interface, Unmarshallable. You will see *Unmarshallable.java* among the generated source files. While this interface is always the same, generating it allows Zeus classes to be unnecessary for runtime operation of the *web.xml* generated classes.

The rest of these interfaces and classes should be familiar to any SAX guru; DefaultHandler and LexicalHandler are SAX-defined classes and interfaces. They allow this class to handle processing of an XML file on its own, without any sort of external framework. Independence from an external framework allows Zeus-generated classes to become unfettered from Zeus itself. Looking further through the source reveals a lot of methods like this:

```
public void characters(char[] ch, int start, int len)
    throws SAXException {

    // Feed this to the correct ContentHandler
    Unmarshallable current = getCurrentUNode( );
    if (current != this) {
        current.characters(ch, start, len);
        return;
    }

    String text = new String(ch, start, len);
    text = text.trim( );
    if (zeus_inDisplayName) {
        if (this.displayName == null) {
            this.displayName = text;
        } else {
            this.displayName =
            new StringBuffer(this.displayName).append(text).toString( );
        }
        return;
    }

    if (zeus_inDescription) {
        if (this.description == null) {
            this.description = text;
        } else {
            this.description =
            new StringBuffer(this.description).append(text).toString( );
        }
        return;
    }
}

public void fatalError(SAXParseException e) throws SAXException {
    if ((validate) && (!hasDTD)) {
        throw new SAXException("Validation is turned on, but no DTD has been"
            "specified in the input XML document. Please supply a"
            "DTD through a DOCTYPE reference.");
    }
    if (errorHandler != null) {
        errorHandler.fatalError(e);
    }
}
public void endDTD( ) throws SAXException {
    // Currently no-op
}
```

These are, of course, SAX callback methods. You can walk through this code and see that, at unmarshalling, this class is actually handed to the SAX parser as the instance of the SAX ContentHandler to use in parsing. It is also set as the lexical handler, which allows the classes to deal with DTD declarations and other lexical events. Then, the classes themselves (starting with the top-level WebApp class) handle delegation of SAX calls to the nested element classes. The result is an implementation that runs as fast as SAX allows, while remaining self-contained. If you're working with a mobile device or hardware with a very limited memory capacity, this makes Zeus ideal due to its small footprint. The *zeus.jar* archive can be left off of the device completely.

 If all that talk about ContentHandlers, lexical events, and SAX confused you, don't worry too much about it. You don't have to know the internals of SAX to use a data binding package. However, you may want to pick up a copy of my book *Java and XML* (O'Reilly) to review these concepts.

Ant Taskdef

You may also have wondered if there is any easier way to deal with class generation. Typing in long commands with a lot of options can be tedious, and you will probably end up writing your own scripts and tools to handle this task for you. However, Zeus provides the ability to run class generation as an Ant task, which will be helpful for those of you already using Ant as a build tool.

Once you have built Zeus (or downloaded it in binary form), you have everything you need to use this task definition. First, you will need to add the following lines to your build file, enabling Ant to find this task definition:

```
<taskdef name="zeus" classname="org.enhydra.zeus.util.ZeusTask">
  <classpath>
    <pathelement path="${path.to.zeus.jar}" />
    <pathelement path="${path.to.dtdparser.jar}" />
    <pathelement path="${path.to.xerces.jar}" />
  </classpath>
</taskdef>
```

Be sure to replace the highlighted section with the path to your Zeus and related classes. You can then use the zeus task, which behaves identically to the command-line version of the class generation tool:

```
<zeus sourceDir="ch07/src/xml" destDir="ch07/src/generated">
  <constraint type="DTD"
              constraintFile="web-app_2_2.dtd"
              javaPackage="javajaxb.generated.web"
              collapseSimpleElements="true"
              ignoreIDAttributes="true"
  />
</zeus>
```

The only difference here is that you need to specify the constraint type (DTD is used here), which allows future constraint-type support by this same task. You can also nest multiple constraint elements within the zeus tag, allowing you to handle multiple DTDs through one task; however, this requires all processed DTDs to be generated into the same output directory. If you want to use different input or output directories, you will need to use multiple instances of the zeus task.

Here's the completed Ant target, which generates the source code and then compiles the generated source. In fact, this is the exact Ant target used to build this chapter's samples:

```
<target name="ch07" depends="prepare">
  <!-- Set up Zeus taskdef -->
  <taskdef name="zeus" classname="org.enhydra.zeus.util.ZeusTask">
    <classpath>
      <pathelement path="${zeus}" />
      <pathelement path="${dtdparser}" />
      <pathelement path="${xerces}" />
    </classpath>
  </taskdef>

  <zeus sourceDir="ch07/src/xml" destDir="ch07/src/generated">
    <constraint type="DTD"
                constraintFile="web-app_2_2.dtd"
                javaPackage="javajaxb.generated.web"
                collapseSimpleElements="true"
                ignoreIDAttributes="true"
    />
  </zeus>
  <javac srcdir="ch07/src/generated"
         destdir="${build.dir}"
         debug="${debug}"
         optimize="${optimize}"
         includes="**/*.java" />
</target>
```

This Ant task should make your life much easier and avoid needless typing repetitions of long command-line options.

While this may have seemed like a whirlwind tour, you now have all the information you need to use Zeus in your own programs. You should also understand how Zeus differs from JAXB and when each might be an appropriate solution. In the next chapter, I'll show you another open source data binding package: Exolab's Castor.

CHAPTER 8

Castor

The next package I want to visit is Castor, from the Exolab group. Like Zeus, Castor is a free, open source package that provides XML-to-Java data binding, as well as several other additional features discussed later. The project is hosted at *http://castor.exolab.org* and is one of the oldest data binding projects around. As a result, it has a lot of maturity, which provides stability and a rich feature set. On the downside, it was around long before JAXB, so there are some significant differences in how it functions as compared to JAXB. That said, it remains an excellent choice for data binding when JAXB support is not required.

Process Flow

Castor follows the basic process flow outlined in the first six chapters. However, like Zeus, it deviates from this basic path to support some additional feature sets. Furthermore, Castor was developed before JAXB was more than a twinkling in Sun's eye and therefore had to come up with original solutions for many problems that are fairly standardized now. This section looks at how Castor deals with class generation, marshalling, and unmarshalling.

Class generation in Castor is handled through a utility class, `org.xml.castor.xml.SourceGenerator`. This class functions much like JAXB's schema compiler (xjc) and Zeus's `DTDSourceGenerator` class. As a result, you should already be familiar with how this process works. An input XML constraint set is supplied, along with several options like a Java package, a destination directory, and collection types. The output is a set of source files that can be compiled and used in your Java programs.

The primary difference in the handling of class generation in Castor, though, is in the generated classes themselves. Remember that in both JAXB and Zeus, the generated classes contained all necessary code to operate in Java, as well as information about the XML document the class came from. Therefore, you might have member variables like `name` and `id` relating to Java, and member variables like `namespaceURI` and `elementName` relating to the XML the class unmarshals from. Castor works on a segregation principle, splitting the XML information from the Java information. The result is two classes for each XML object: the first, named after the element (such as *Employee.java*), and the second, a *class descriptor* (such as *EmployeeDescriptor.java*). This class descriptor stores XML information like namespace mappings, validation data, and the XML names of the elements and attributes for the object. These class descriptors are then used at marshalling and unmarshalling time to properly convert the Java object to and from XML. The result, from a class generation standpoint, is the process shown in Figure 8-1.

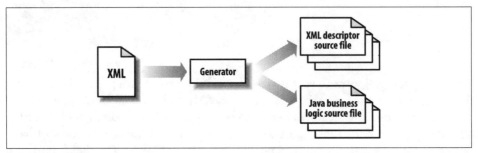

Figure 8-1. Class generation in Castor

Marshalling and unmarshalling in Castor is handled almost identically to JAXB. The Castor-generated classes import several classes in the core Castor package, particularly in the org.xml.castor.xml package. Then these Castor classes handle marshalling and unmarshalling, returning the results through the generated classes. These Castor classes use the data in the Java object, along with the metadata in the class descriptors, to handle this conversion. Figure 8-2 diagrams the process in detail.

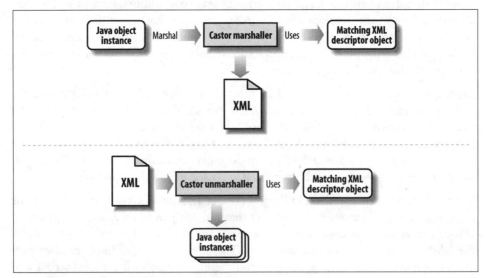

Figure 8-2. Marshalling and unmarshalling in Castor

Installation and Setup

Getting Castor set up for use is just as simple as setting up Zeus; after a download and some classpath manipulation, you are ready to go. First, visit the Castor download site at *http://castor.exolab.org/download.html*, and download the Castor package. As of this writing, the latest version was 0.9.3.9, so the download file was called *castor-0.9.3.9.tgz* or *castor-0.9.3.9.zip*. Several other options for downloading are worth mentioning:

castor-0.9.3.9.jar
> The Castor *jar* files without any tools or examples

castor-0.9.3.9-xml.jar
> For use if you need only XML data binding, without any of Castor's other mapping features

castor-0.9.3.9-doc.tgz
> A complete set of Castor documentation, including relevant specifications; handy for reference purposes

Once you've got the archive, you'll want to expand it into a working directory so you can access the samples and command-line tools. You'll then need to add the Castor library to your classpath:

```
C:\dev\castor> set CLASSPATH=%CLASSPTH%;c:\dev\castor\castor-0.9.3.9.jar
```

Also make sure you have an XML parser in your classpath; I used *xerces.jar* in these examples. There are several other libraries in the Castor download, but you will not need any of them for XML data binding. However, if you plan to work with Castor's Java Data Objects (JDO) capabilities (see the end of this chapter for more details), then you will also need to add *jdbc-se2.0.jar* and *jta1.0.1.jar* to your classpath.

Additionally, you will want to download the Apache regular expressions processor. This is used by Castor to handle pattern matching in XML Schema and is available online at *http://jakarta.apache.org/site/binindex.html*. Download the latest release version, extract the archive (*jakarta-regexp-1.2.jar*), and add it to your classpath as well. Once that's taken care of, you are ready to use Castor's data binding facilities.

Class Generation

Class generation in Castor is similar in operation to both JAXB and Zeus; you use a helper class to pass in a set of XML constraints, and the result is source code that can then be compiled and used in your programs. This section details the constraint models that can be used by Castor, as well as the options that Castor makes available beyond what you have already seen in JAXB.

DTDs

Oddly enough, Castor is exactly the opposite of most available data binding packages. Instead of supporting DTDs and having a fairly immature XML Schema implementation, Castor began with support for XML Schema. Because of the work involved in supporting the ever-changing XML Schema specification, and perhaps because of a lack of interest, Castor has never provided support for class generation from DTDs. If you need to support class generation from DTDs, you will need to use one of the other data binding packages discussed previously.

XML Schema

While DTDs are not supported by Castor, excellent support for XML Schema is included. Because Castor has worked on schemas for quite a while, the project has a rich feature set for dealing with that language. The basic class you will use for schema-to-Java generation is `org.exolab.castor.builder.SourceGenerator`.

Castor includes a script, *sourceGen.bat* and *sourceGen* (for Windows and Unix, respectively), with the Castor download. However, this script has incorrect paths in it and does not work properly. Instead of using this script, simply follow the instructions in this section. By the time you read it, the fix will probably be back in the open source project's code base anyway.

Before dealing with usage of that class, you will need an XML Schema to convert to Java. Here, I use a schema that is a simple representation of a human resources database. This could be used for storing information in static XML documents and then later converted into an actual database model. Example 8-1 shows this schema.

Example 8-1. HR database constraint model

```
<?xml version="1.0"?>
<xsd:schema xmlns:xsd="http://www.w3.org/2001/XMLSchema"
    targetNamespace="http://www.oreilly.com/catalog/javajaxb">

  <xsd:annotation>
    <xsd:documentation>This is a simple HR database in XML.</xsd:documentation>
  </xsd:annotation>

  <!-- Employee Storage -->
  <xsd:element name="employees">
    <xsd:complexType>
      <xsd:sequence>
        <xsd:element ref="employee" maxOccurs="unbounded" />
      </xsd:sequence>
    </xsd:complexType>
  </xsd:element>

  <!-- Employee -->
```

Example 8-1. HR database constraint model (continued)

```xsd
<xsd:element name="employee">
  <xsd:annotation>
    <xsd:documentation>Employee representation</xsd:documentation>
  </xsd:annotation>
  <xsd:complexType>
    <xsd:sequence>
      <xsd:element name="name" type="xsd:string" />
      <xsd:element ref="address" maxOccurs="2" />
      <xsd:element ref="organization" />
      <xsd:element ref="office" />
    </xsd:sequence>
    <xsd:attribute name="id" type="xsd:integer" />
  </xsd:complexType>
</xsd:element>

<!-- Organization -->
<xsd:element name="organization">
  <xsd:complexType>
    <xsd:sequence>
      <xsd:element name="name" type="xsd:string"/>
    </xsd:sequence>
    <xsd:attribute name="id" type="xsd:integer" />
  </xsd:complexType>
</xsd:element>

<!-- Office -->
<xsd:element name="office">
  <xsd:complexType>
    <xsd:sequence>
      <xsd:element ref="address"/>
    </xsd:sequence>
    <xsd:attribute name="id" type="xsd:integer" />
  </xsd:complexType>
</xsd:element>

<!-- Address -->
<xsd:element name="address">
  <xsd:complexType>
    <xsd:sequence>
      <xsd:element name="street1" type="xsd:string"/>
      <xsd:element name="street2" type="xsd:string" minOccurs="0"/>
      <xsd:element name="city" type="xsd:string"/>
      <xsd:element name="state" type="stateAbbreviation"/>
      <xsd:element ref="zip-code"/>
    </xsd:sequence>
  </xsd:complexType>
</xsd:element>

<xsd:element name="zip-code">
  <xsd:simpleType>
    <xsd:restriction base="xsd:string">
      <xsd:pattern value="[0-9]{5}(-[0-9]{4})?"/>
    </xsd:restriction>
```

Example 8-1. HR database constraint model (continued)

```
      </xsd:simpleType>
    </xsd:element>

    <xsd:simpleType name="stateAbbreviation">
  <xsd:restriction base="xsd:string">
        <xsd:pattern value="[A-Z]{2}"/>
    </xsd:restriction>
    </xsd:simpleType>
</xsd:schema>
```

 If you are unfamiliar with XML Schema or unsure about some features in this example, you may want to refer to *XML in a Nutshell* (O'Reilly), by Elliotte Rusty Harold and W. Scott Means, for more information.

With your schema in place, you are ready to use Castor's class generation tools. Here's the basic command needed to generate classes:

```
/dev/javajaxb/ch08/src $ java org.exolab.castor.builder.SourceGenerator \
    -i xml/hr.xsd \
    -package javajaxb.generated.hr \
    -dest generated
```

The result is what you should expect by now: several source files in the specified directory. Several other options available for this tool are summarized in Table 8-1.

Table 8-1. Castor SourceGenerator options

Flag	Value	Purpose
-i	Filename of constraints	Specifies constraint set to Castor.
-package	Java package	Sets package for generated classes.
-dest	Destination directory	Specifies the directory to put generated classes in.
-line-separator	unix or mac or win	Sets line separator to use for a specific platform. By default, this will attempt to autodetect your platform.
-f	N/A	Hides nonfatal warnings in class generation.
-h	N/A	Displays a help screen and command usage.
-verbose	N/A	Displays extra information about the class generation process.
-nodesc	N/A	Prevents creation of class descriptors.
-types	Type for collections	Specifies the collection type to use.
-nomarshall	N/A	Prevents generation of marshall( ) methods on generated classes.
-testable	N/A	Sets up class to be usable by the Castor testing framework (included with Castor).

Most of these options are self-explanatory. Note that with the -normashall flag, it is possible to create a set of read-only objects. This was discussed in some detail in Chapter 6, so shouldn't be anything new to you.

The -nodesc option is worthy of note. As we've seen, Castor cleanly divides the Java code for working with XML data from the Java code that deals directly with XML. As a result, you will see that each class (such as Address), has a descriptor with a similar name (AddressDescriptor). The first has all of your basic accessor and mutator methods, while the second stores namespace information, validation methods, and so forth. By omitting this file, you lose the ability to do effective round-tripping, in which your input XML document can be unmarshalled and then immediately marshaled back out to an exact duplicate of the input file. Instead, you'll get the correct XML data but lose valuable information like namespaces, validation, and other data specific to the class descriptors. Unless you've got a good reason to drop this (like a tiny memory footprint to deal with), avoid using this option.

Another option is the -types argument. By default, JDK 1.1–compliant collection types, such as java.util.Vector, are used. However, if you prefer that Java 2 Collection types be used, you can specify j2 as the value for this argument:

```
/dev/javajaxb/ch08/src $ java org.exolab.castor.builder.SourceGenerator \
    -i xml/hr.xsd \
    -package javajaxb.generated.hr \
    -dest generated
    -types j2
```

In this command, the -types option ensures that java.util.List types are used instead of Vectors.

Once you have generated classes (preferably with class descriptors and Java 2 collections), you can compile those classes and move on to marshalling and unmarshalling.

Unmarshalling and Marshalling

At this point, marshalling and unmarshalling should be pretty routine. As in the last chapter, I'll skip over application-specific business logic and move right to dealing with the actual marshal() and unmarshal() methods. You'll see that the same principles, and sometimes even commands, used in JAXB and Zeus apply to Castor as well.

You'll also need an XML document that corresponds to the HR XML Schema detailed earlier. Example 8-2 is such a document and is used throughout the rest of this chapter.

Example 8-2. HR instance document

```
<?xml version="1.0"?>

<employees>
  <employee id="2673">
    <name>Bobby Jones</name>
    <address>
      <street1>289 Running Brook Lane</street1>
      <city>Stanchion</city>
      <state>TX</state>
```

Example 8-2. HR instance document (continued)

```
      <zip-code>79021</zip-code>
    </address>
    <organization id="24">
      <name>Billing</name>
    </organization>
    <office id="56">
      <address>
        <street1>112 Murdock</street1>
        <street2>Suite 2101</street2>
        <city>Millford</city>
        <state>TX</state>
        <zip-code>79025</zip-code>
      </address>
    </office>
  </employee>

  <employee id="10982">
    <name>Cindy Cunningham</name>
    <address>
      <street1>1400 Sandy Lake Road</street1>
      <street2>Appartment 4D</street2>
      <city>Boston</city>
      <state>MA</state>
      <zip-code>20967</zip-code>
    </address>
    <organization id="11">
      <name>Marketing</name>
    </organization>
    <office id="12">
      <address>
        <street1>1800 Cambridge Drive</street1>
        <city>Boston</city>
        <state>MA</state>
        <zip-code>20968</zip-code>
      </address>
    </office>
  </employee>
</employees>
```

Save this document as *hr.xml*, and you are ready to unmarshal it to Java.

Unmarshalling

The actual process of converting from XML to Java is simple; having done this twice now (with Zeus and JAXB), Example 8-3 should not present anything too surprising. Take a look at the code; oddities are noted after the listing.

Example 8-3. Unmarshalling with Castor

```
package javajaxb;

import java.io.File;
```

Example 8-3. Unmarshalling with Castor (continued)

```java
import java.io.FileReader;
import java.io.IOException;

// Castor
import org.exolab.castor.xml.MarshalException;
import org.exolab.castor.xml.ValidationException;

// Generated hr.xml classes
import javajaxb.generated.hr.*;

public class EmployeeLister {

    /** The descriptor to read in */
    private File descriptor;

    /** The output file to write to */
    private File outputFile;

    /** The object tree read in */
    private Employees employees;

    public EmployeeLister(File descriptor, File outputFile) {
        employees = null;
        this.descriptor = descriptor;
        this.outputFile = outputFile;
    }

    public void list(boolean validate)
        throws IOException, MarshalException, ValidationException {

        // Unmarshall
        employees = Employees.unmarshal(new FileReader(descriptor));

        // Do some basic printing
        System.out.println("--- Employee Listing ---\n");
        Employee[] employeeList = employees.getEmployee();
        for (int i=0; i<employeeList.length; i++) {
            Employee employee = employeeList[i];
            System.out.println("Employee: " + employee.getName());
            System.out.println("Organization: " +
                employee.getOrganization().getName());
            System.out.println("Office: " +
                employee.getOffice().getAddress().getCity() + ", " +
                employee.getOffice().getAddress().getState() + "\n");
        }
    }

    public static void main(String[] args) {
        try {
            if (args.length != 2) {
                System.out.println("Usage: java javajaxb.EmployeeLister " +
                    "[web.xml filename] [output.xml filename]");
                return;
```

Example 8-3. Unmarshalling with Castor (continued)

```
        }

        EmployeeLister lister =
            new EmployeeLister(new File(args[0]), new File(args[1]));
        lister.list(true);
    } catch (Exception e) {
        e.printStackTrace();
    }
  }
}
```

First note the different exceptions that Castor throws: org.exolab.castor.xml. ValidationException and org.exolab.castor.xml.MarshalException. It is a bit odd that the unmarshalling process can throw a MarshalException, but that exception is used for all marshalling and unmarshalling problems in Castor.

I've also chosen to use the getEmployee() method, which returns a typed array (Employee[]). This allows quick, type-safe iteration through the values in the list of employees. You could also use the enumerateEmployee() method, which returns a java.util.Enumeration for a different means of iteration over the Employee objects. Either approach works in essentially the same way.

Once you see how to get access to the objects, simply printing out values should be old news. You can also examine the generated classes for other available methods, although they are similar to what you've already seen in previous chapters.

Marshalling

Marshalling in Castor is equally simple. You'll use the marshal() method, in conjunction with a provided Java Writer. Here's a modified EmployeeLister to deal with making some changes and writing those changes out to a new file:

```
package javajaxb;

import java.io.File;
import java.io.FileReader;
import java.io.FileWriter;
import java.io.IOException;

// Castor
import org.exolab.castor.xml.MarshalException;
import org.exolab.castor.xml.ValidationException;

// Generated hr.xml classes
import javajaxb.generated.hr.*;

public class EmployeeLister {

    // Existing methods
```

```java
    public void modify( )
        throws IOException, MarshalException, ValidationException {
        // Add a new employee
        Employee employee = new Employee( );
        employee.setName("Ben Rochester");
        Address address = new Address( );
        address.setStreet1("708 Teakwood Drive");
        address.setCity("Flower Mound");
        address.setState("TX");
        address.setZipCode("75028");
        employee.addAddress(address);

        Organization organization = new Organization( );
        organization.setId(43);
        organization.setName("Technical Services");
        employee.setOrganization(organization);

        Office office = new Office( );
        office.setId(241);
        Address officeAddress = new Address( );
        officeAddress.setStreet1("1202 Business Square");
        officeAddress.setStreet2("Suite 302");
        officeAddress.setCity("Dallas");
        officeAddress.setState("TX");
        officeAddress.setZipCode("75218-8921");
        office.setAddress(officeAddress);
        employee.setOffice(office);

        // Add employee to list
        employees.addEmployee(employee);

        // marshal
        employees.marshal(new FileWriter(outputFile));
    }

    public static void main(String[] args) {
        try {
            if (args.length != 2) {
                System.out.println("Usage: java javajaxb.EmployeeLister " +
                    "[web.xml filename] [output.xml filename]");
                return;
            }

            EmployeeLister lister =
                new EmployeeLister(new File(args[0]), new File(args[1]));
            lister.list(true);
            lister.modify( );
        } catch (Exception e) {
            e.printStackTrace( );
        }
    }
}
```

You'll see the same basic procedures followed as those used with both JAXB and Zeus. You'll also see two Castor-specific exceptions (MarshalException and ValidationException). This latter exception is responsible for reporting problems that arise when the data is converted to XML. For example, make the following change to the modify() method:

```java
public void modify()
    throws IOException, MarshalException, ValidationException {
    // Add a new employee
    Employee employee = new Employee();
    employee.setName("Ben Rochester");
    Address address = new Address();
    address.setStreet1("708 Teakwood Drive");
    address.setCity("Flower Mound");
    address.setState("TX");
    address.setZipCode("75028");
    employee.addAddress(address);
    /*
    Organization organization = new Organization();
    organization.setId(43);
    organization.setName("Technical Services");
    employee.setOrganization(organization);
    */
    Office office = new Office();
    office.setId(241);
    Address officeAddress = new Address();
    officeAddress.setStreet1("1202 Business Square");
    officeAddress.setStreet2("Suite 302");
    officeAddress.setCity("Dallas");
    officeAddress.setState("TX");
    officeAddress.setZipCode("75218-8921");
    office.setAddress(officeAddress);
    employee.setOffice(office);

    // Add employee to list
    employees.addEmployee(employee);

    // marshal
    employees.marshal(new FileWriter(outputFile));
}
```

Running EmployeeLister now results in the following exception:

```
[java] ValidationException: organization is a required field.;
[java]    - location of error: XPATH: employees/employee
[java]      at org.exolab.castor.xml.FieldValidator.validate(FieldValidator.
          java:196)
[java]       at org.exolab.castor.xml.util.XMLClassDescriptorImpl.validate
          (XMLClassDescriptorImpl.java:740)
[java]      at org.exolab.castor.xml.Validator.validate(Validator.java:118)
[java]      at org.exolab.castor.xml.FieldValidator.validate(FieldValidator.
          java:217)
[java]       at org.exolab.castor.xml.util.XMLClassDescriptorImpl.validate
          (XMLClassDescriptorImpl.java:740)
```

```
[java]        at org.exolab.castor.xml.Validator.validate(Validator.java:118)
[java]        at org.exolab.castor.xml.Marshaller.validate(Marshaller.java:1221)
[java]        at org.exolab.castor.xml.Marshaller.marshal(Marshaller.java:536)
[java]        at org.exolab.castor.xml.Marshaller.marshal(Marshaller.java:460)
[java]        at javajaxb.generated.hr.Employees.marshal(Employees.java:138)
```

Castor's marshalling process realizes that the organization element is required, and because no data is supplied for that element, the Java objects cannot be marshaled into XML. This will ensure that your resultant XML documents are always valid with regard to the original XML Schema structure used for class generation.

Mapping Files

Like JAXB, Castor provides the equivalent of a binding schema. These schemas are called *mapping files* in Castor, but serve the same purpose as they do in JAXB. They allow you to control the transformation of names from XML to Java and back again. An element in an XML document called emp could be unmarshalled into a Java class called Employee, and a method variable in Java named address1 might be marshaled back to XML as the name street1.

Because you have already seen how these files work in JAXB and because Castor uses many of the same semantics, I'm going to give you the basic syntax and let you play with the permutations on your own. Perhaps the best reference on these files is the DTD Castor supplied; it can be found online at *http://Castor.exolab.org/mapping.dtd*. Rather than going through each option, look at Example 8-4. This example is a complete mapping file that converts from the Java-generated classes shown earlier in this chapter to an entirely new XML format.

Example 8-4. A Castor mapping file for the HR classes

```xml
<?xml version="1.0"?>
<!DOCTYPE mapping PUBLIC "-//EXOLAB/Castor Object Mapping DTD Version 1.0//EN"
                        "http://Castor.exolab.org/mapping.dtd">

<mapping>
  <class name="javajaxb.generated.hr.Employees">
    <map-to xml="emp-list"/>
    <field name="Employee"
           type="javajaxb.generated.hr.Employee">
      <bind-xml name="emp" />
    </field>
  </class>

  <class name="javajaxb.generated.hr.Employee">
    <field name="Id"
           type="integer">
      <bind-xml name="emp-id" node="attribute"/>
    </field>
    <field name="name"
           type="java.lang.String">
```

Example 8-4. A Castor mapping file for the HR classes (continued)

```
      <bind-xml name="emp-name" node="attribute"/>
    </field>
    <field name="Address"
          type="javajaxb.generated.hr.Address">
      <bind-xml name="emp-address" />
    </field>
    <field name="Organization"
          type="javajaxb.generated.hr.Organization">
      <bind-xml name="emp-org"/>
    </field>
    <field name="Office"
          type="javajaxb.generated.hr.Office">
      <bind-xml name="emp-office"/>
    </field>
  </class>

  <class name="javajaxb.generated.hr.Address">
    <field name="Street1"
          type="java.lang.String">
      <bind-xml name="line-1" node="element"/>
    </field>
    <field name="Street2"
          type="java.lang.String">
      <bind-xml name="line-2" node="element"/>
    </field>
    <field name="City"
          type="java.lang.String">
      <bind-xml name="city" node="element"/>
    </field>
    <field name="State"
          type="java.lang.String">
      <bind-xml name="state" node="element"/>
    </field>
    <field name="ZipCode"
          type="java.lang.String">
      <bind-xml name="zip-code" node="element"/>
    </field>
  </class>

  <class name="javajaxb.generated.hr.Office">
    <field name="Id"
          type="integer">
      <bind-xml name="office-id" node="attribute"/>
    </field>
    <field name="Address"
          type="javajaxb.generated.hr.Address">
      <bind-xml name="office-address" node="element"/>
    </field>
  </class>

  <class name="javajaxb.generated.hr.Organization">
    <field name="Id"
          type="integer">
```

Example 8-4. A Castor mapping file for the HR classes (continued)

```
      <bind-xml name="org-id" node="element"/>
    </field>
    <field name="Name"
           type="java.lang.String">
      <bind-xml name="org-name" node="element"/>
    </field>
  </class>
</mapping>
```

I think that you'll find this format very intuitive. The core of the mappings is the `class` element. For each `class` element, you then specify the name of the Java class being mapped through the `name` attribute. Then, you will need to specify a number of `field` elements for each class; each element represents the mapping of a class member variable to an XML element or attribute. You supply the name of the field, the type of that field, and the XML name to bind to. You can also specify whether the XML construct will be an attribute or element through the use of the `node` attribute on the `bind-xml` element. Again, the format should be apparent when you look at the mapping file.

Note that nothing special was required to handle the lists within the `Employees` and `Employee` objects (the former has a list of employees and the latter a list of addresses). By specifying that these field mappings are normal, Castor takes care of figuring out what to do with these lists. The only thing to be aware of is that you should use the variable name (`EmployeeList`) without the `List` portion of the name (resulting in just `Employee`); otherwise, Castor will report that the mapping file is invalid.

With this mapping file in place, it's possible to modify the example class, `EmployeeLister`, to write out the employee database to this new format. Since a lot has changed, I've given this modified example a new listing number, Example 8-5.

Example 8-5. EmployeeLister with mapping code

```
package javajaxb;

import java.io.File;
import java.io.FileReader;
import java.io.FileWriter;
import java.io.IOException;

// Castor
import org.exolab.castor.mapping.Mapping;
import org.exolab.castor.mapping.MappingException;
import org.exolab.castor.xml.MarshalException;
import org.exolab.castor.xml.Marshaller;
import org.exolab.castor.xml.ValidationException;

// Generated hr.xml classes
import javajaxb.generated.hr.*;
```

Example 8-5. EmployeeLister with mapping code (continued)

```
public class EmployeeLister {

    /** The descriptor to read in */
    private File descriptor;

    /** The output file to write to */
    private File outputFile;

    /** The converted output file */
    private File convertFile;

    /** The object tree read in */
    private Employees employees;

    /** Change this for your location! */
    private static final String MAPPING_FILENAME =
        "c:/dev/javajaxb/ch08/src/xml/mapping.xml";

    public EmployeeLister(File descriptor, File outputFile, File convertFile) {
        employees = null;
        this.descriptor = descriptor;
        this.outputFile = outputFile;
        this.convertFile = convertFile;
    }

    public void list(boolean validate)
        throws IOException, MarshalException, ValidationException {

        // Unmarshall
        employees = Employees.unmarshal(new FileReader(descriptor));

        // Do some basic printing
        System.out.println("--- Employee Listing ---\n");
        Employee[] employeeList = employees.getEmployee();
        for (int i=0; i<employeeList.length; i++) {
            Employee employee = employeeList[i];
            System.out.println("Employee: " + employee.getName());
            System.out.println("Organization: " +
            employee.getOrganization().getName());
            System.out.println("Office: " +
                employee.getOffice().getAddress().getCity() + ", " +
                employee.getOffice().getAddress().getState() + "\n");
        }
    }

    public void modify()
        throws IOException, MarshalException, ValidationException {
        // Add a new employee
        Employee employee = new Employee();
        employee.setName("Ben Rochester");
        Address address = new Address();
```

Example 8-5. EmployeeLister with mapping code (continued)

```
        address.setStreet1("708 Teakwood Drive");
        address.setCity("Flower Mound");
        address.setState("TX");
        address.setZipCode("75028");
        employee.addAddress(address);

        Organization organization = new Organization( );
        organization.setId(43);
        organization.setName("Technical Services");
        employee.setOrganization(organization);

        Office office = new Office( );
        office.setId(241);
        Address officeAddress = new Address( );
        officeAddress.setStreet1("1202 Business Square");
        officeAddress.setStreet2("Suite 302");
        officeAddress.setCity("Dallas");
        officeAddress.setState("TX");
        officeAddress.setZipCode("75218-8921");
        office.setAddress(officeAddress);
        employee.setOffice(office);

        // Add employee to list
        employees.addEmployee(employee);

        // marshal
        employees.marshal(new FileWriter(outputFile));
    }

    public void convert( )
        throws IOException, MarshalException, ValidationException, MappingException {

        // Load up the mapping information
        Mapping mapping = new Mapping( );
        mapping.loadMapping(MAPPING_FILENAME);

        // Marshall using that information
        Marshaller marshaller = new Marshaller(new FileWriter(convertFile));
        marshaller.setMapping(mapping);
        marshaller.marshal(employees);
    }

    public static void main(String[] args) {
        try {
            if (args.length != 3) {
                System.out.println("Usage: java javajaxb.EmployeeLister " +
                    "[web.xml filename] [output.xml filename] [convert.xml filename]");
                return;
            }

            EmployeeLister lister =
                new EmployeeLister(new File(args[0]), new File(args[1]),
                                new File(args[2]));
```

Example 8-5. EmployeeLister with mapping code (continued)

```
          lister.list(true);
          lister.modify( );
          lister.convert( );
      } catch (Exception e) {
          e.printStackTrace( );
      }
   }
}
```

The portions of this code that read in and wrote out the original XML document are unchanged. However, a new method has been added, and this method writes out the employee information using the mapping file from Example 8-4:

```
// Load up the mapping information
Mapping mapping = new Mapping( );
mapping.loadMapping(MAPPING_FILENAME);

// Marshall using that information
Marshaller marshaller = new Marshaller(new FileWriter(convertFile));
marshaller.setMapping(mapping);
marshaller.marshal(employees);
```

This code is also pretty self-explanatory. A mapping is created, and then the mapping file to be used is loaded up. You will need to catch a MappingException, which indicates whether any parsing errors occur while reading the mapping. Then you see that the employee instance is marshalled back out. However, the Castor org.exolab. castor.xml.Marshaller object is used this time, instead of operating upon the employee instance directly. That allows you to set a mapping to use in the conversion to XML through the setMapping( ) method. Finally, marshal( ) is called and the Java objects are written out as XML (using the mapping information).

If you compile and run this program (and change the MAPPING_FILENAME constant to point to your own mapping file location), you get the XML document shown in Example 8-6. This document has all the information present in the original XML documents, but in a completely different format.

Example 8-6. Converted HR XML document

```
<?xml version="1.0"?>
<emp-list>
  <emp emp-id="2673" emp-name="Bobby Jones">
    <emp-address>
      <line-1>289 Running Brook Lane</line-1>
      <city>Stanchion</city>
      <state>TX</state>
      <zip-code>79021</zip-code>
    </emp-address>
    <emp-org>
      <org-id>24</org-id>
      <org-name>Billing</org-name>
    </emp-org>
```

Example 8-6. Converted HR XML document (continued)

```
    <emp-office office-id="56">
      <office-address>
        <line-1>112 Murdock</line-1>
        <line-2>Suite 2101</line-2>
        <city>Millford</city>
        <state>TX</state>
        <zip-code>79025</zip-code>
      </office-address>
    </emp-office>
  </emp>
  <emp emp-id="10982" emp-name="Cindy Cunningham">
    <emp-address>
      <line-1>1400 Sandy Lake Road</line-1>
      <line-2>Appartment 4D</line-2>
      <city>Boston</city>
      <state>MA</state>
      <zip-code>20967</zip-code>
    </emp-address>
    <emp-org>
      <org-id>11</org-id>
      <org-name>Marketing</org-name>
    </emp-org>
    <emp-office office-id="12">
      <office-address>
        <line-1>1800 Cambridge Drive</line-1>
        <city>Boston</city>
        <state>MA</state>
        <zip-code>20968</zip-code>
      </office-address>
    </emp-office>
  </emp>
  <emp emp-name="Ben Rochester">
    <emp-address>
      <line-1>708 Teakwood Drive</line-1>
      <city>Flower Mound</city>
      <state>TX</state>
      <zip-code>75028</zip-code>
    </emp-address>
    <emp-org>
      <org-id>43</org-id>
      <org-name>Technical Services</org-name>
    </emp-org>
    <emp-office office-id="241">
      <office-address>
        <line-1>1202 Business Square</line-1>
        <line-2>Suite 302</line-2>
        <city>Dallas</city>
        <state>TX</state>
        <zip-code>75218-8921</zip-code>
      </office-address>
    </emp-office>
  </emp>
</emp-list>
```

You can see what a powerful tool this is; conversion between differing XML formats becomes simple by reading in data in one format and writing it out to another.

 You can also use these mapping files for unmarshalling and convert from one XML format to a different Java format. The process is almost identical, and you will want to use the org.exolab.castor.xml. Unmarshaller class for this purpose:

```
Unmarshaller unmarshaller = new Unmarshaller(myMapping);
Employees employees = (Employees)unmarshaller.
unmarshal(myInputSource);
```

Additional Features

Castor offers several additional features that are not present in JAXB (or any other open source data binding package); these features are centered around mapping between other data formats and Java. For example, Castor allows you to map database objects and LDAP queries—in addition to XML documents—to Java. This is obviously a book on XML data binding, so I'll touch on these topics only briefly here; however, you may find that you need a package that provides APIs for SQL, LDAP, and XML. If that is the case, Castor is an excellent choice.

Database and Directory Server Mappings

Castor allows mapping between databases and directory servers to Java, as well as the standard XML-to-Java mappings discussed in this chapter and the rest of this book. This obviously makes it easier to work with these non-Java structures, particularly when a similar API can be used for XML, LDAP, and databases. The result is data source transparency, which allows your code to switch easily from an XML store to a database or from a database to a directory server.

These mappings are accomplished through simple XML mapping files, like the one shown here:

```
<!DOCTYPE databases PUBLIC "-//EXOLAB/Castor Mapping DTD Version 1.0//EN"
                    "http://castor.exolab.org/mapping.dtd">
<mapping>

  <!-- Mapping for Employees -->
  <class name="javajaxb.generated.Employee"
         identity="id">
    <description>A Company Employee</description>
    <map-to table="EMPLOYEES" xml="employee" />
    <field name="id" type="integer" >
      <sql name="id" type="integer"/>
      <xml node="attribute"/>
    </field>
    <field name="name" type="string">
      <sql name="name" type="char" dirty="check" />
```

```
        <xml node="text" />
      </field>
      <field name="organization" type="javajaxb.generated.Organization">
        <sql name="organization_id" />
        <xml name="organization" node="element" />
      </field>
    </class>
  </mapping>
```

Here, the EMPLOYEES table is mapped to the generated Java object Employee (the same one detailed above, which also worked for XML). For each field, the SQL field name is described, the XML node type (element, attribute, or character data [text]) is specified, and the XML name is given. This results in a simple mapping from SQL tables to Java objects. Of course, this mapping must be used in a process that communicates between the database or directory and Java. In Castor, this process is called JDO.

JDO

JDO stands for Java Data Objects. Castor provides support for JDO through the org. exolab.castor.jdo package. More specifically, JDO is being used increasingly as a lightweight alternative to Enterprise JavaBeans (EJBs). While it does not offer the advanced transactional and security framework that EJB containers provide, JDO can be an attractive solution for lightweight database applications or Intranet applications in which data integrity is not as important as in commercial or financial applications. JDO also offers an arguably more powerful interface to databases, as it is simple to execute SQL queries directly and quickly operate upon them. While the developer must maintain responsibility for the data being manipulated, JDO generally provides more control than do CMP entity beans.

 I made a lot of general statements in that last paragraph, and you should take them as such. A good EJB programmer can use both container and bean-managed persistence to overcome all limitations, just as a bad JDO programmer can completely wreck a database. Of course, the converse is also true. Before deciding that JDO will replace EJBs and ripping out your J2EE infrastructure, take some time to study JDO; it will save you headaches down the line.

Using JDO in Castor is as simple as importing several Castor JDO classes and creating an XML configuration file for the database to connect to. Such a configuration file might look like this:

```
<database name="humanResources" engine="oracle">
  <driver class-name="oracle.jdbc.driver.OracleDriver"
          url="jdbc:oracle:thin:@hr.myCompany.com:8723:HRDB">
    <param name="user" value="admin" />
    <param name="password" value="passwd" />
  </driver>
  <mapping href="employees.xml" />
```

```
        <mapping href="organizations.xml" />
        <mapping href="offices.xml" />
    </database>
```

This file specifies the JDBC driver to use, as well as connection information for the database. It also specifies several mapping files that map database structures to Java, as detailed above. With that file in place, you could then use code, as seen here, to access and update a database:

```
public void transfer(int employeeId, int organizationId) throws Exception {
    // Create JDO object and configure it
    JDO jdo = new JDO("oracleDatabase");
    jdo.setConfiguration("oracleDatabaseConfig.xml");

    // Open up the database and begin a transaction
    Database oracleDB = jdo.getDatabase( );
    oracleDB.begin( );

    // Build query to find specified employee
    Query selectQuery = oracleDB.getQuery(
        "SELECT emp FROM EMPLOYEES emp WHERE employeeId=$");
    selectQuery.bind(employeeId);

    // Execute and transfer the employee
    QueryResults empRecord = selectQuery.execute( );
    Employee employee = (Employee)empRecord.next( );
    employee.setOrganizationId(organizationId);

    // Commit and close up
    oracleDB.commit( );
    oracleDB.close( );
}
```

Here, an employee is retrieved from an Oracle database, and then his organization is changed to the value specified to the transfer( ) method. I've kept the example simple, but you should get the idea. As you can see, this is a particularly useful means of dealing with databases; it takes the best of JDBC and adds some usability. Also note that the objects in the database have been bound to objects (the EMPLOYEES table rows are turned into Employee object instances). In this way, Java idioms are maintained even when working with databases.

What really begins to add value to this proposition is the ability to then convert from this database format directly to XML. For example, it is simple to convert the employee object instance that you modified the organization for into an XML document:

```
    // Execute and transfer the employee
    QueryResults empRecord = selectQuery.execute( );
    Employee employee = (Employee)empRecord.next( );
    employee.setOrganizationId(organizationId);

    // Convert to XML
    Marshaller.marshal(employee, myOutputStream);
```

This probably seems almost too easy to be possible, but it's exactly what you might see in a common Castor program. The resulting XML would look something like this:

```xml
<?xml version="1.0"?>
<employee id="8903">
  <name>Bob Oldhouse</name>
  <address>
    <street1>908 Gageway Drive</street1>
    <city>Mesquite</city>
    <state>TX</state>
    <zip-code>75150</zip-code>
  </address>
  <organization id="15">
    <name>Information Systems</name>
  </organization>
  <office id="41">
    <address>
      <street1>1712 East Longview Road</street1>
      <city>Mesquite</city>
      <state>TX</state>
      <zip-code>75149</zip-code>
    </address>
  </office>
</employee>
```

This looks just like the XML used in the rest of the chapter, except that this XML has a root element of employee, instead of employees. That's because you marshalled an instance of the Employee class, rather than the Employees class. Still, this easy conversion from a database to XML and back should get your mind whirring about Castor's possibilities.

As in the case of Zeus, this chapter was another lightning-fast tour through a data binding package. However, as stated before, the intent is to familiarize you with these packages so you can make your own decisions. If you worked through the first six chapters, data binding should be a breeze now; you only need to apply the specific semantics of a package to use XML data in your Java applications with ease. In the next chapter, I'll complete the trio of open source package by examining Quick, which offers a unique approach to handling data binding tasks.

CHAPTER 9

Quick

At this point, you probably are getting a little tired of seeing data binding package after data binding package scrolled across the screen. That's good if you are; it means that you really have a handle on what data binding is. It also should reflect the ease with which you can switch between different data binding conceptual models (switching the code is a bit tougher, mind you). With an hour of free time, some Javadoc, and the examples in the preceding chapters, you should be able to use any of the covered projects in your own programming tasks.

With all that said, then, you are probably wondering why there is yet another chapter on a data binding framework. The answer is simple: Quick is entirely different from what you have seen so far. While Quick is free for use and released as open source, it is based on entirely different concepts. While it allows conversion between Java and XML, it is not a data binding framework, at least in the sense of the JAXB definition of the term. You'll learn exactly why this is so in this chapter and also see when it is worthwhile to deviate from the data binding standard and use a package like Quick.

Process Flow

I'll spend a lot of time in this section, as the concepts that underlie Quick are fundamentally different from those that underlie JAXB and the data binding frameworks we have looked at so far. One striking difference is that comparisons between JAXB and Quick easily become meaningless, as the processes involved are very different. However, you should take note of the divergences in methodology (using the Quick Java Markup Language (QJML) instead of DTDs, for example) and understand how they have their own places in XML-based programming projects.

Quick Versus JAXB

Quick is geared primarily at converting from XML to existing Java classes. While it has the ability to generate Java classes (something I'll cover later in the chapter), it's initial goal is to map data between one data format and another. Thinking about Quick as a mapping technology, in fact, may be the best way to begin to distinguish it from the data binding frameworks discussed so far.

Remember that when using JAXB, the first step was always to define a DTD. This step presumed that the data you were working with was going to be converted to Java from the outset and that you could structure the XML element and attribute names in a way that made sense to a programmer (the XML element purchase became the Java object Purchase, for example). While this is certainly tractable for new projects, it is not always so for projects that have been running for months or years. In these cases, you are more likely to have XML documents that look like Example 9-1.

Example 9-1. A confusing purchase order

```
<?xml version="1.0"?>
<po>
  <o id="23" s_id="145-9876-90">
    <p_name>OfficeConnect Ethernet Hub 4</p_name>
    <m_name>3Com</m_name>
    <p_c>149.99</p_c>
    <sk oh="true" num="22" />
  </o>
  <o id="24" s_id="145-9873-23">
    <p_name>OfficeConnect ISDN Lan Modem</p_name>
    <m_name>3Com</m_name>
    <p_c>229.99</p_c>
    <sk oh="true" num="3" />
  </o>
  <o id="51" s_id="124-6334-04">
    <p_name>Orinoco Residential Gateway</p_name>
    <m_name>Lucent</m_name>
    <p_c>499.99</p_c>
    <sk oh="false" num="28" />
  </o>
</po>
```

The meaning of these element and attribute names is pretty unclear. Generating Java classes from this document's DTD would be essentially useless, as no business meaning would result. While some meaning can be assumed from the data, the Java classes (PO and O, for example) would be essentially useless. What you really want is the set of classes shown in Figure 9-1, which have names that make more sense.

At this point, you're probably thinking about the wonders of binding schemas and how they would allow you to map the element po to the class PurchaseOrder, sk to InStock, and so on). This is a good idea, and makes sense; however, let me throw a wrench in the works. Assume you have a couple of hundred, or even thousand, XML documents like those I've shown here in your system. Then, in a process of sweeping reform by new management, you're ordered to convert this document to a more readable form, such as the one shown in Example 9-2.

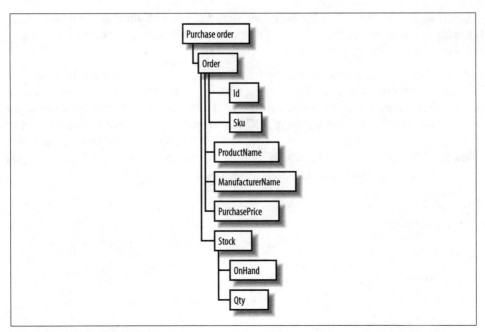

Figure 9-1. Classes for an XML document

Example 9-2. A more readable purchase order

```
<?xml version="1.0"?>

<purchaseOrder>
  <order id="23" sku="145-9876-90">
    <productName>OfficeConnect Ehternet Hub 4</productName>
    <manufacturerName>3Com</manufacturerName>
    <purchasePrice>149.99</purchasePrice>
    <stock onHand="true" qty="22" />
  </order>
  <order id="24" sku="145-9873-23">
    <productName>OfficeConnect ISDN Lan Modem</productName>
    <manufacturerName>Lucent</manufacturerName>
    <purchasePrice>229.99</purchasePrice>
    <stock onHand="true" qty="3" />
  </order>
  <order id="51" sku="124-6334-04">
    <productName>Orinoco Residential Gateway</productName>
    <manufacturerName>3Com</manufacturerName>
    <purchasePrice>499.99</purchasePrice>
    <stock onHand="false" qty="28" />
  </order>
</purchaseOrder>
```

Now you've got *two* different XML formats that are represented by *one* set of Java objects. How do you ensure that both types of XML can be converted to the single set of Java objects, without running into all sorts of class generation issues with mismatches and the like? The answer, of course, is Quick.

> It is possible to achieve this same result using a combination of XSLT and one of the other data binding frameworks. You could preprocess the XML by applying an XML transformation and then use data binding on the resultant transformed XML. However, this is a lot of work and processing power to expend on a solution that Quick provides right out of the box. Castor provides similar functionality, as you saw through the use of the mapping file.

Instead of handling the mapping of XML names to Java ones at class generation, Quick handles them at runtime and during marshalling and unmarshalling. The result is that several different XML document formats can all be converted into the same set of Java classes. This can be extremely handy in the situation I've outlined, or whenever transformation should take place during Java-to-XML or XML-to-Java conversion, rather than at class generation time.

> I realize that some people, especially those new to the world of XML, may think that this scenario is contrived. On the contrary, I have been at numerous companies where early XML-based systems use XML formats that are incredibly terse. Because XML is a verbose language, early authors often would condense element and attribute names to "decrease the size" of the XML document. However, as XML has become more popular and transmission mediums have improved, these documents, as well as new ones, have been written in a much more readable format. Still, the old XML documents are often kept for archival and historical purposes. The result is the very scenario I've outlined.

When you put the pieces together, you end up with the process flow shown in Figure 9-2.

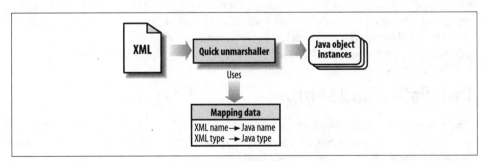

Figure 9-2. Data conversion using Quick

Performance Considerations

With this change in process, you will need to take into account some performance differences. First, there is a significantly smaller up-front cost. You can avoid generating classes from your DTDs; in fact, you can even avoid writing DTDs (although I don't recommend that approach). You also don't have to worry about making your generated classes available to other groups or companies that may interact with your XML documents. The result is that the interchange of data in this manner is about as simple as is possible.

Keep in mind that you will pay some performance penalties at runtime, though. The data binding packages examined previously have the instructions for converting between Java and XML coded and compiled into bytecode in the form of generated classes. This means that conversion is generally pretty fast. With the Quick approach, this transformation happens at runtime and involves a mapping file. The result is that the Quick engine has to parse that mapping file and interpret it at every conversion. This adds time to your conversion. However, you gain a good deal of flexibility with that performance hit, so it is often well worth the cost.

As has already been mentioned, the key becomes determining when to use a traditional data binding package and when to use Quick. You've already seen some scenarios in which Quick shines; anytime heterogeneous data formats must all be tied to a single Java format, it becomes an excellent choice. It's also ideal when you need to exchange data with other companies that you don't have much contact with; rather than having to coordinate on a set of generated classes, Quick allows data binding without dealing with versioning issues across companies (when you have one version of generated classes and the other company has another).

Finally, it's quite reasonable to use both data binding packages (JAXB, Zeus, or Castor) and Quick. For example, you may have a case in which traditional data binding approaches work very well. Then, however, you need to run some reports based on existing Java objects. Quick would allow you to take your XML data and map it to the report objects, without reworking all your existing code based on another set of generated classes. The possibilities quickly become limitless; simply use the best tool for the job, and experiment with multiple solutions if you aren't sure what is appropriate.

Installation and Setup

The process of installing these frameworks is fairly similar. You will need to visit *http://jxquick.sourceforge.net* online and locate the Quick downloadable archive. At the time of this writing, that file was called *Quick4.3.0.zip*. You should open this file and extract its contents into a directory you can work from, such as *c:\dev\Quick4* or *~/dev/Quick4*. There are two directories of immediate interest to you: *Quick4/BATs* and *Quick4/JARs*. The first contains utility programs that will be used in common Quick tasks and should be added to your PATH environment variable. The second contains a number of libraries you will need; add each to your CLASSPATH environment variable.

 If you already have an XML parser in your CLASSPATH variable, such as *xerces.jar*, you can skip adding the included *crimson.jar* library.

When you're finished, your CLASSPATH should look something like this:

```
C:\dev\javajaxb\ch09\src\xml>echo %CLASSPATH%
c:\dev\toolsTech\Zeus\lib\xerces.jar;c:\dev\Quick4\JARs\dtdparser113.jar;
c:\dev\Quick4\JARs\Quick4rt.jar;c:\dev\Quick4\JARs\Quick4util.jar
```

Once these libraries and batch files are accessible, you are ready to move on to marshalling and unmarshalling.

Unmarshalling and Marshalling

Now that you have a basic understanding of what Quick does, you're ready to learn how to use it. This section will cover conversion to and from XML using Quick and demonstrate the mapping features that it provides. Because Quick is a bit different from the other data binding frameworks, I recommend that you work through this section in order.

Unmarshalling

The first step in getting things going with Quick is to ensure you have a DTD on hand. That DTD will be the basis for generating some files that Quick needs in order to operate.

 It is possible to use Quick by creating a Quick-specific data schema for modeling constraints directly. However, you can't validate against this sort of schema, and you can't exchange it with others who don't know Quick. For that reason, it is *always* better to start with a DTD, which is universally understood, and use Quick's tools to convert that DTD to Quick-specific formats.

Have Java classes on hand

Because the typical Quick processing cycle doesn't involve generation of Java classes, you should have these classes available. Rather than take up a lot of space in this chapter, I've placed the source for a sample set of classes in Appendix B. You can type these in from the appendix or download them from the book's web site at *http://www.newInstance.com*. In either case, you will want to compile them and make them available to your applications for conversion to and from Java.

Converting DTDs to QDML

Example 9-3 shows the DTD for the document from Example 9-1.

Example 9-3. DTD for Example 9-1

```
<!ELEMENT po (o+)>

<!ELEMENT o (p_name, m_name, p_c, sk)>
<!ATTLIST o
        id    CDATA    #REQUIRED
        s_id  CDATA    #REQUIRED
>

<!ELEMENT p_name (#PCDATA)>
<!ELEMENT m_name (#PCDATA)>
<!ELEMENT p_c (#PCDATA)>
<!ELEMENT sk EMPTY>
<!ATTLIST sk
        oh    (true | false)    "true"
        num   CDATA    #REQUIRED
>
```

This DTD is pretty basic and provides the constraint set for the XML document to convert to Java. However, as already mentioned, Quick doesn't understand DTDs—at least not for use in conversion. Thus, you need to convert your DTD into a Quick Document Markup Language (QDML) schema. This is just another schema language, but is much simpler to work with than XML Schema. Quick provides a tool for converting DTDs in the set of batch files called *cfgDtd2Qdml*.

 All of the batch files mentioned here exist in both the Windows *.bat* format and the Unix *.sh* format. Use the appropriate version for your platform.

You need to specify the input DTD to process, using the -in parameter, and the output filename to use for the QDML file, with the -out parameter. Use this utility to create a QDML document for your purchase order DTD:

```
C:\dev\javajaxb\ch09\src\xml>cfgDtd2Qdml -in=po.dtd -out=po.qdml

C:\dev\javajaxb\ch09\src\xml>call cfg.bat
    classpath:///com/jxml/quick/util/dtd2qdml/dtd2qdml.config
    -in po.dtd -out po.qdml

C:\dev\javajaxb\ch09\src\xml>call quickClasspath.bat
```

Note that only the first statement needs to be entered; the second two are generated by the Quick utility class. When this command completes, you should have a new file, *po.qdml*. Example 9-4 shows the generated Quick schema.

Example 9-4. QDML for Example 9-1

```xml
<?xml version="1.0" encoding="ISO-8859-1"?>
<qdml>
    <bean tag="po">
        <elements>
            <item coin="o" repeating="true"/>
        </elements>
    </bean>
    <bean tag="o">
        <attributes>
            <item coin="o.id"/>
            <item coin="o.s_id"/>
        </attributes>
        <elements>
            <item coin="p_name"/>
            <item coin="m_name"/>
            <item coin="p_c"/>
            <item coin="sk"/>
        </elements>
    </bean>
    <text label="o.id" tag="id"/>
    <text label="o.s_id" tag="s_id"/>
    <text tag="p_name"/>
    <text tag="m_name"/>
    <text tag="p_c"/>
    <bean tag="sk">
        <attributes>
            <item coin="sk.oh" optional="true" value="true"/>
            <item coin="sk.num"/>
        </attributes>
    </bean>
    <text label="sk.oh" tag="oh">
        <enum value="true"/>
        <enum value="false"/>
    </text>
    <text label="sk.num" tag="num"/>
</qdml>
```

This output is itself an XML document. It represents the various values, types, and data that a purchase order can have, and will be used by Quick in the process of conversion to and from Java. It's also significantly less complex than an XML Schema representing the same constraints would be.

I found one bug in the generation of the QDML document; it did not indicate the XML root element. This bug later created errors in QJML Schema generation. To avoid these problems, add in the following attribute to your QDML document's qdml element:

```xml
<?xml version="1.0" encoding="ISO-8859-1"?>
<qdml root="po">
    <!-- The rest stays as is -->
</qdml>
```

Once you have this document, you need to generate a Quick binding schema, abbreviated Quick Java Markup Language (QJML). I realize that you are probably wondering why you need to perform another conversion; however, recall that many Quick users start with a QDML document, bypassing the DTD step altogether. However, as already stated, you should start with a DTD so that you can use that DTD in other XML applications, most of which do not accept Quick markup languages (QDML, QJML, etc.). Besides, all the Quick utilities make this process trivial.

Converting QDML to QJML

You should think of a QJML Schema as a binding schema, much like what was discussed in Chapter 6. This schema lets Quick know how to convert your XML types to Java types and is required for Quick unmarshalling. Like the process of converting a DTD to a QDML document, a simple script handles this task:

```
[bmclaugh@aragorn xml]$ sh cfgQdml2Qjml.sh -in=po.qdml -out=po.qjml \
    -package=javajaxb.po
```

Note that I've also specified the Java package that contains the classes to unmarshal to; this should match your on-hand Java classes. Quick generates its "best guess" at how to convert from XML to Java; however, you will need to go in and make changes to this schema. This is particularly true in the case of rather cryptic XML documents, such as the *po.xml* document. You will want to make changes so that the XML will be marshaled into the more human-readable variables names you are using in your Java classes. Example 9-5 shows the generated QJML schema, along with the changes needed to make it convert easily into the Java classes in Appendix B. I've highlighted the changes that had to be made, so you can see what was left as is from generation and what was hand modified.

Example 9-5. QJML for use in unmarshalling

```
<?xml version="1.0" encoding="ISO-8859-1" standalone="no"?>
<!DOCTYPE qjml SYSTEM "classpath:///qjml.dtd">
<qjml root="po">
    <bean tag="po">
        <targetClass>javajaxb.po.PurchaseOrder</targetClass>
        <elements>
            <item coin="o" repeating="True">
                <property kind="list" name="orderList"/>
            </item>
        </elements>
    </bean>
    <bean tag="o">
        <targetClass>javajaxb.po.Order</targetClass>
        <attributes>
            <item coin="o.id">
                <property name="id"/>
            </item>
            <item coin="o.s_id">
                <property name="sku"/>
```

Example 9-5. QJML for use in unmarshalling (continued)

```
                    </item>
              </attributes>
              <elements>
                    <item coin="p_name">
                          <property name="productName"/>
                    </item>
                    <item coin="m_name">
                          <property name="manufacturerName"/>
                    </item>
                    <item coin="p_c">
                          <property name="purchasePrice"/>
                    </item>
                    <item coin="sk">
                          <property name="stock"/>
                    </item>
              </elements>
        </bean>
        <text label="o.id" tag="id" validInherited="True" type="int" />
        <text label="o.s_id" tag="s_id" validInherited="True" type="PCDATA" />
        <text tag="p_name" validInherited="True" type="PCDATA" />
        <text tag="m_name" validInherited="True" type="PCDATA" />
        <text tag="p_c" validInherited="True" type="float" />
        <bean tag="sk">
              <targetClass>javajaxb.po.Stock</targetClass>
              <attributes>
                    <item coin="sk.oh" optional="True" value="true">
                          <property name="onHand"/>
                    </item>
                    <item coin="sk.num">
                          <property name="quantity"/>
                    </item>
              </attributes>
        </bean>
        <text label="sk.oh" tag="oh" validInherited="True" type="boolean" />
        <text label="sk.num" tag="num" validInherited="True" type="int" />
</qjml>
```

Most changes in the top portion of the file deal with changing the obscure XML names (po, sk, etc.) into the names of the target Java classes and variables (javajaxb. po.Order, purchasePrice, etc.). In the bottom portion of the file, though, you'll see several text elements. Here's what one of them looked like before modification:

```
<text label="o.id" tag="id" validInherited="True">
      <targetClass>javajaxb.po.O_id</targetClass>
</text>
```

As you can see, it specifies a targetClass, which triggers conversion into a user-defined class. However, these values should be converted into Java primitive types; to accomplish this, the targetClass child element is removed and the type attribute is used instead to specify the primitive type. Also note that PCDATA is used to represent a simple String type.

More conversion

You should perform one more conversion at this point. While there are ways to get around this particular conversion, it will ultimately help your performance dramatically. The format that the Quick engine deals with is called Quick Internal Markup Language (QIML) and is optimized for the conversion processes that Quick performs. However, this format is not very human readable (it is XML, but has lots of Quick-specific items in it); therefore QJML is preferred by programmers like you and me for specifying conversion properties.

As a result, using QJML directly results in an internal conversion before every unmarshalling and marshalling process. This, of course, is bad for performance (and Quick already has more runtime lag than other frameworks, in the general case). Therefore, you should perform one more step before coding and convert your QJML file into a QIML one:

```
C:\dev\javajaxb\ch09\src\xml>cfgQjml2Qiml -in=po.qjml -out=po.qiml
```

The result of this transformation is a new file, *po.qiml*. I've chosen not to show this in the text, as it is a rather long listing and has little readable value. You are more than welcome to dig in and look at the file for yourself.

Additionally, you can streamline things even further by turning this schema into a Java source file and then compiling it. In other words, you remove the responsibility for creating bytecode from the Quick engine. You can actually manage to make Quick perform as fast as other frameworks with this final step. Not surprisingly, Quick has a utility for this, too! Here's what you will need to do:

```
C:\dev\javajaxb\ch09\src\xml>cfgQiml2Java -in=po.qiml
    -class=javajaxb.po.PurchaseOrderSchema
    -key=po.qjml
    -out=..\java\javajaxb\po\PurchaseOrderSchema.java
```

The value for the key parameter is the name of the QJML schema that is represented. The class parameter is the name of the Java class to generate; note that this accepts a fully qualified Java class name. Finally, I've dropped this class in with my existing Java source files from Appendix B. You should make sure that these classes, including this new generated class, are all compiled; then you are ready to write some code.

Unmarshalling

I realize that you've worked hard to get to unmarshalling. However, this work needs to occur only once, since once you have your QDML, QJML, and QIML, you never need to create them again. You are now ready to write code that actually utilizes these files and converts your XML document into Java-accessible data.

Everything in Quick is based around the `com.jxml.quick.QDoc` class, which represents QIML schemas and XML documents. You will create and operate this class using the `com.jxml.quick.Quick` class, which provides several static utility and parsing methods. Example 9-6 shows unmarshalling in action using these two classes.

Example 9-6. Unmarshalling using Quick

```java
package javajaxb;

import java.io.File;
import java.io.IOException;
import java.util.Iterator;

// Quick classes
import com.jxml.quick.QDoc;
import com.jxml.quick.Quick;

// SAX classes
import org.xml.sax.SAXException;

// The PO user-defined classes
import javajaxb.po.*;

public class PurchaseOrderViewer {

    /** The descriptor to read in */
    private File inputFile;

    /** The output file to write to */
    private File outputFile;

    /** The QJML schema in Java format */
    private QDoc purchaseOrderSchema;

    /** The QDoc for the purchase order */
    private QDoc purchaseOrderDoc;

    /** The object tree */
    private PurchaseOrder purchaseOrder;

    public PurchaseOrderViewer(File inputFile, File outputFile) {
        this.inputFile = inputFile;
        this.outputFile = outputFile;
    }

    public void view(boolean validate) throws Exception {
        // Instantiate the QIML class object
        purchaseOrderSchema = PurchaseOrderSchema.createSchema();

        // Unmarshal
        purchaseOrderDoc =
            Quick.parse(purchaseOrderSchema, inputFile.getAbsolutePath());

        // Get the object tree
        purchaseOrder = (PurchaseOrder)Quick.getRoot(purchaseOrderDoc);

        // Do some printing
        System.out.println("Purchase Order:");
        for (Iterator i = purchaseOrder.getOrderList().iterator(); i.hasNext(); ) {
```

Example 9-6. Unmarshalling using Quick (continued)

```
            Order order = (Order)i.next();
            System.out.println(" * Order (ID=" + order.getId() + ", SKU=" +
                order.getSku() + "):");
            System.out.println("   + Product Name: " + order.getProductName());
            System.out.println("   + Manufacturer Name: " +
                order.getManufacturerName());
            System.out.println("   + Purchase Price: $" +
                order.getPurchasePrice());

            Stock stock = order.getStock();
            System.out.println("   + Quantity Ordered: " + stock.getQuantity());
            System.out.println("   + Order Total: $" +
                (order.getPurchasePrice() * stock.getQuantity()));
        }
        System.out.println("Total Order Cost: $" + purchaseOrder.getTotalPrice());
    }

    public static void main(String[] args) {
        try {
            if (args.length != 2) {
                System.out.println("Usage: java javajaxb.PurchaseOrderViewer " +
                    "[po.xml filename] [output.xml filename]");
                return;
            }

            PurchaseOrderViewer viewer =
                new PurchaseOrderViewer(new File(args[0]), new File(args[1]));
            viewer.view();
        } catch (Exception e) {
            e.printStackTrace();
        }
    }
}
```

As you can see, the first step is to get an instance of the QIML schema in Java object form. This is accomplished through the use of the createSchema() method on that class, which you generated in the last section. The result of this operation is that schema in QDoc object format.

You then use that schema as the first argument in the parse() method of the Quick class. This method expects a QIML schema object to use for mapping and then (as a second object) the filename or URI of the XML document to parse and convert. The result of this operation is another QDoc instance, although this time it will contain the data from your XML document in object form. To get the actual object tree out of this QDoc, simply call getRoot(), another utility method in the Quick class, and cast the resulting object to your tree type. In the example, this means casting to PurchaseOrder.

Once you have your object tree (the PurchaseOrder object instance), you can operate upon the class in standard fare. I've mixed using the data methods (getQuanity() and getManufacturerName()) with the business method (getTotalPrice()), and the difference is invisible to the programmer. I realize that the means by which unmarshalling was performed were quite a bit different than anything you have seen so far. However, once you get used to the different steps, it will feel much more natural. To help make things clearer, Figure 9-3 shows the unmarshalling process and ties each step to the relevant method invocations.

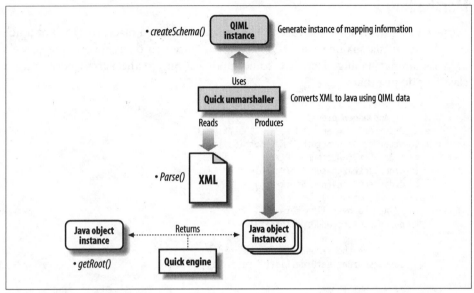

Figure 9-3. Quick unmarshalling

You can compile this class and run it, supplying the XML document shown in Example 9-1 as input. Your results should look like this:

```
[java] Purchase Order:
[java]  * Order (ID=23, SKU=145-9876-90):
[java]     + Product Name: OfficeConnect Ethernet Hub 4
[java]     + Manufacturer Name: 3Com
[java]     + Purchase Price: $149.99
[java]     + Quantity Ordered: 22
[java]     + Order Total: $3299.78
[java]  * Order (ID=24, SKU=145-9873-23):
[java]     + Product Name: OfficeConnect ISDN Lan Modem
[java]     + Manufacturer Name: 3Com
[java]     + Purchase Price: $229.99
[java]     + Quantity Ordered: 3
[java]     + Order Total: $689.97003
[java]  * Order (ID=51, SKU=124-6334-04):
[java]     + Product Name: Orinoco Residential Gateway
[java]     + Manufacturer Name: 3Com
[java]     + Purchase Price: $499.99
[java]     + Quantity Ordered: 28
[java]     + Order Total: $13999.72
[java] Total Order Cost: $17989.469
```

I've run my sample from within Ant (the downloadable examples are all in this format), so you may not see the [java] prefix to each line of your own output. If you have any problems, make sure that you have the required classes in your classpath, and try again.

Marshalling

Because you already have the various Quick-specific files in place, there is not much complexity in marshalling using Quick. All you need to do is reverse the process used for unmarshalling. Here are some modifications to the PurchaseOrderViewer class that do just that:

```java
public void modify() throws Exception {
    // Add a new order
    Order order = new Order(77, "990-7716-23");
    order.setManufacturerName("Toshiba");
    order.setProductName("PCX1100U Cable Modem");
    order.setPurchasePrice(new Float(87.98).floatValue());
    order.setStock(new Stock(30));

    // Add to overall order
    purchaseOrder.addOrder(order);

    // Remove the second item in the order
    purchaseOrder.getOrderList().remove(1);

    // Marshal to XML
    Quick.express(purchaseOrderDoc, outputFile.getAbsolutePath());
}

public static void main(String[] args) {
    try {
        if (args.length != 2) {
            System.out.println("Usage: java javajaxb.PurchaseOrderViewer " +
                "[po.xml filename] [output.xml filename]");
            return;
        }

        PurchaseOrderViewer viewer =
            new PurchaseOrderViewer(new File(args[0]), new File(args[1]));
        viewer.view();
        viewer.modify();
    } catch (Exception e) {
        e.printStackTrace();
    }
}
```

I've obviously included only portions of the class that were modified, so be sure to leave the rest of the class unchanged.

As in previous examples, normal methods on classes—instead of XML- or data binding-specific methods—were used. Then, the express() method was used on the

Quick class for marshalling out to XML. The arguments are the document to express and the filename to write to.

 A common mistake is to pass this method your object tree; in this case, that would be the PurchaseOrder instance itself. You should remember, though, that Quick's conversion facilities are all external to the business classes, so a PurchaseOrder instance has no idea about how to convert itself into XML. Instead, you need to pass in a QDoc instance.

Once you have made these changes, recompile and run your example. You should get an output XML document that looks like Example 9-7.

Example 9-7. Output from PurchaseOrderviewer

```
<?xml version="1.0" encoding="ISO-8859-1"?>
<po>
    <o id="23" s_id="145-9876-90">
        <p_name>OfficeConnect Ethernet Hub 4</p_name>
        <m_name>3Com</m_name>
        <p_c>149.99</p_c>
        <sk num="22" oh="True"/>
    </o>
    <o id="51" s_id="124-6334-04">
        <p_name>Orinoco Residential Gateway</p_name>
        <m_name>3Com</m_name>
        <p_c>499.99</p_c>
        <sk num="28" oh="False"/>
    </o>
    <o id="77" s_id="990-7716-23">
        <p_name>PCX1100U Cable Modem</p_name>
        <m_name>Toshiba</m_name>
        <p_c>87.98</p_c>
        <sk num="30" oh="True"/>
    </o>
</po>
```

As you can see, the new order was added successfully, and the second item in the list was removed. Once again, through a simple example, you should be able to understand and use Quick in your own programs. Other than these few simple methods (parse(), express(), getRoot()), you need to be familiar with only Quick's utilities for type conversion (DTD to QDML, QIML to Java, etc.).

Format Conversion

As mentioned in the beginning of this chapter, one of Quick's major payoffs is the ability to convert between differing XML formats and a single set of Java objects. Lest you miss this ability in relation to Quick, I want to run through that process here. This will explain how to convert the XML document in Example 9-2 into the Java classes from Appendix B.

The easiest way to accomplish this task is to *not* go all the way back to the DTD stage. There is no need to start with a DTD for that format, as you already have a QJML file that specifies the Java names to convert to. Instead, you will want to copy and edit this file to use the different XML names; however, the Java names should be left as is. Example 9-8 shows this new file.

Example 9-8. Converting XML formats using QJML

```
<?xml version="1.0" encoding="ISO-8859-1" standalone="no"?>
<!DOCTYPE qjml SYSTEM "classpath:///qjml.dtd">
<qjml root="purchaseOrder">
    <bean tag="purchaseOrder">
        <targetClass>javajaxb.po.PurchaseOrder</targetClass>
        <elements>
            <item coin="order" repeating="True">
                <property kind="list" name="orderList"/>
            </item>
        </elements>
    </bean>
    <bean tag="order">
        <targetClass>javajaxb.po.Order</targetClass>
        <attributes>
            <item coin="order.id">
                <property name="id"/>
            </item>
            <item coin="order.sku">
                <property name="sku"/>
            </item>
        </attributes>
        <elements>
            <item coin="productName">
                <property name="productName"/>
            </item>
            <item coin="manufacturerName">
                <property name="manufacturerName"/>
            </item>
            <item coin="purchasePrice">
                <property name="purchasePrice"/>
            </item>
            <item coin="stock">
                <property name="stock"/>
            </item>
        </elements>
    </bean>
    <text label="order.id" tag="id" validInherited="True" type="int" />
    <text label="order.sku" tag="sku" validInherited="True" type="PCDATA" />
    <text tag="productName" validInherited="True" type="PCDATA" />
    <text tag="manufacturerName" validInherited="True" type="PCDATA" />
    <text tag="purchasePrice" validInherited="True" type="float" />
    <bean tag="stock">
        <targetClass>javajaxb.po.Stock</targetClass>
        <attributes>
            <item coin="stock.onHand" optional="True" value="true">
```

Example 9-8. Converting XML formats using QJML (continued)

```
                <property name="onHand"/>
          </item>
          <item coin="stock.qty">
                <property name="quantity"/>
          </item>
      </attributes>
   </bean>
   <text label="stock.onHand" tag="onHand" validInherited="True" type="boolean" />
   <text label="stock.qty" tag="qty" validInherited="True" type="int" />
</qjml>
```

This conversion is fairly simple; each time the old format's XML name is shown, simply change it to read as the XML name is in the new format. You can then run through the similar process of creating a Java compiled object from this QJML schema:

```
C:\dev\javajaxb\ch09\src\xml>cfgQjml2Qiml -in=purchaseOrder.qjml -out=purchaseOrder.
qiml

C:\dev\javajaxb\ch09\src\xml>cfgQiml2Java -in=purchaseOrder.qiml
-class=javajaxb.po.PurchaseOrderSchema2
-key=purchaseOrder.qjml
-out=..\java\javajaxb\po\PurchaseOrderSchema2.java
```

This will generate a new QIML file for this schema, and then a Java source file for conversion between this new format and your existing Java classes.

Be sure to use different filenames than the ones already shown in this chapter (I used *purchaseOrder* and PurchaseOrderSchema2 here). Otherwise, you will overwrite your existing files and have all sorts of odd bugs show up.

Once you compile the PurchaseOrderSchema2 class, you can simply use it instead of the original class, PurchaseOrderSchema, and you'll convert between formats with ease.

Additional Features

Like the other data binding frameworks, Quick has several additional features that are useful. Some of these features may turn out to be exactly what you need and will help you decide whether Quick is useful for your own programming needs.

Class Generation

As mentioned earlier, Quick does not consider class generation from DTDs a standard part of its process flow. However, it does provide class generation, which is useful when using Quick in more traditional data binding applications. For the process to work, you will need a QJML binding schema, such as the one shown in Example 9-5. Of course, any modifications you need to make to ensure correct mappings should be made before starting the process. Once you've got your QJML schema set up as you like it, you can use the `cfgQjml2Java` script to generate Java classes:

```
C:\dev\javajaxb\ch09\src\xml>cfgQjml2Java -in=po.qjml -out=..\generated

C:\dev\javajaxb\ch09\src\xml>call cfg.bat
    classpath:///com/jxml/quick/util/qjml2java/qjml2java.config
    -in po.qjml -out ..\generated

C:\dev\javajaxb\ch09\src\xml>call quickClasspath.bat
creating directories for ..\generated\javajaxb\po\PurchaseOrder.java
new file: ..\generated\javajaxb\po\PurchaseOrder.java
new file: ..\generated\javajaxb\po\Order.java
new file: ..\generated\javajaxb\po\Stock.java
```

This is pretty basic and shouldn't be too confusing after already having used JAXB, Zeus, and Castor. You can then compile these classes and use them in your application. This is useful when you have a desire to use Quick and need to generate skeleton classes for your application. You can add business logic and additional methods to these classes, and as long as the generated method signatures are not changed, Quick will work with the modified classes.

QDML to DTD

You may find that, over time, you begin to prefer using QDML to DTDs. This is particularly true for those who may have XML Schema experience, as QDML is closer to that format than to DTDs. If this is the case, and you end up writing QDML directly (bypassing writing a DTD first), Quick can help. As you will almost certainly need DTDs at some point (for validation, data exchange, or any number of other reasons), you may need to convert your QDML to DTD. It is here that Quick can help, as it provides a utility to do just that:

```
[bmclaugh@aragorn xml]$ sh cfgQdml2Dtd.sh -in=po.qdml -out=po_from_qdml.dtd
```

You can view the resulting DTD and notice that it is an exact match to the original *po.dtd* shown in Example 9-3 (with some change in ordering). This utility may help if you create your own QDML from scratch or if you need to convert someone else's QDML into a DTD.

CHAPTER 10

Looking Forward

Before closing up shop on data binding, I want to talk briefly about what you should expect in the coming months and years. Data binding is an API that is so new that there is far more ahead for it than there is behind. Because of that, I'm asked far more often about when this feature will be available or when that version will be released than about existing functionality.

While there is certainly a good basis of fact behind all of the predictions in this chapter, you should never consider them ironclad. If you don't already know, deadlines and promises in the technical world are rarely worth the cost of the paper they are printed on. You can consider the information in this chapter reliable, but don't get too hung up on the generalized dates I've tried to provide on when you should see them.

JAXB

JAXB remains the significant focus of most developers just getting into data binding. Because Sun has led the Java charge from the beginning, many programmers who would not use an open source data binding API are finally jumping on board with the JAXB early-access release, which came out in the summer of 2001. This section tries to address some of the frequent questions I get about JAXB and how its development is shaping up.

Final Release

More often than anything else, I'm asked when the JAXB 1.0 release will be publicly available. Since this signifies to many the coming of age of data binding, it is an important question. As noted in this book, several features in the early-access release of JAXB are not complete, and the specification is listed only as Version 0.21 as of this book's writing. The unfortunate answer to "When will JAXB 1.0 be out?" is "I don't know." I was unable to get a solid answer from Sun on this one, so I cannot provide any hard dates.

In terms of functionality, you should expect the 1.0 release to add little in terms of new features from what is outlined in the current JAXB specification (the 0.21 version). While features not implemented in the early access will be in place (for example, the constructor keyword in binding schemas), there is no indication of a major change from what is outlined now. While that may be disappointing if you are looking for this or that particular item to appear, it is also helpful for application planning. You can code your applications to the current JAXB specification and early-access reference implementation and expect to make few changes when a final version of the release surfaces.

Schema Support

Right after the question about JAXB's release date, I'm almost always questioned about XML Schema support in JAXB. Again, you might be disappointed in the answer. JAXB 1.0 has no indication (at least that I've been able to find) of including schema support and will instead focus on DTD support. Again, this is probably disappointing to many, but I would certainly rather see solid DTD support than shaky support for DTDs and XML Schema. Once the framework is in place for DTD class generation, adding XML Schema support should be relatively straightforward, so a point release with schema support is a reasonable expectation; for example, JAXB 1.1 may add schema support to the 1.0 release.

The most notable change that will accompany schema support will be some change or augmentation in how binding schemas function. Because XML Schemas allow type specification, as well as advanced features like pattern matching and extension, binding schemas can often be in conflict with what is specified in an XML Schema. It's unclear how these sorts of conflicts will be resolved or how much of the XML Schema 1.0 specification will be supported by a JAXB schema-aware release. I would not try and use JAXB with XML Schema until a mature release is available; if you need XML Schema support today, your best bet is to check out one of the open source packages that supports XML Schema for constraint models.

Alternate Implementations

While you shouldn't expect to see a lot of change between the early-access release of JAXB and its final version, the other data binding implementations detailed in this book most likely *will* undergo significant changes in the coming months. Any time Sun releases a specification (like JAXB), hordes of programmers begin to write applications to these specifications. As a result, alternate data binding implementations will probably move toward this same specification, allowing interoperability and easy migration for JAXB-based applications. Additionally, it is easier to add functionality to existing bases, like the JAXB specification, than to try to compete with a completely different approach toward data binding.

JAXB Conformance

First, expect a movement in alternate data binding implementations toward the JAXB specification. This isn't as likely a case of suddenly seeing javax.bind packages in open source projects as it is of movement toward the JAXB-defined binding schema. Keep in mind that hundreds of programmers will not touch data binding until JAXB goes into a 1.0 final version, and that within months of that version, there will be literally thousands of binding schemas floating around on programmers' desktops. At this point, enough effort will have been put into those schemas that reworking them for another implementation would be close to impossible.

The result is that developers who want to try another implementation will have a high cost of entry. They will have to rewrite binding schemas and rewrite code to account for changes in these binding schemas. Even open source savvy alpha geeks have to justify time spent in migration to a pointy-haired boss. The result is that even if additional features and performance are available in an alternate implementation, a developer will be hard pressed to get the time and resources to test it out.

As a result, any framework that wants to encourage experimentation among shops already looking at JAXB will want to provide an easy migration path. While Quick will most likely stick with the schema language it defines, the APIs that generate classes in a fashion similar to JAXB (Castor and Zeus) will most likely move to binding schemas. I would be surprised if these APIs did not quickly move to a format that is a superset of the existing binding schema used by JAXB. They can then allow developers easy migration from their existing JAXB-generated classes to their own framework, without requiring changes in the binding schemas already written for JAXB. Instead, they would simply offer additional features.

Overlaying Functionality

While data binding implementations will most likely gravitate toward a common binding schema specification, they will also expand their feature sets. Castor, for example, offers data binding for XML into databases and LDAP stores. Zeus plans to offer binding for not only XML Schema, but also for Relax NG schemas. Quick has a completely unique structure in place, as you saw in Chapter 9. As these frameworks settle on a common interface, they will also stretch to provide features that make them attractive over the standard JAXB framework.

You should expect to see two variations in this added functionality. First, frameworks will provide entirely new directions in supported feature sets. An example of this is Castor LDAP bindings. This is orthogonal to XML data binding, so it doesn't overlap with the XML data binding processes. You'll probably have to learn a new form of binding schema, employ some different marshalling and unmarshalling techniques, and in many cases, learn a new tool. This isn't by any means a bad thing; it is simply movement in a direction different than that of data binding. The second direction is overlaying functionality, which is where things tend to get interesting. An example of this functionality would be in Zeus allowing specification of a separate package for interfaces and implementation classes. This is achieved through constructs in the binding schema that are added to the base set of features that JAXB defines.

What is interesting about this overlaid set of features is that it makes migration *back* to JAXB difficult. As soon as you utilize these additional features, you have changed your binding schema and added keywords (for example, `interfacePackage` or `implPackage`) that JAXB doesn't support. However, this turns out to not be such a bad thing. As long as the additional features that frameworks add are not too obscure, they can result in JAXB adding in the same features. This creates a bit of a community standardization process, albeit over time. Once JAXB adds in these additional features, the alternate implementations will make sure that the element names match up, and suddenly your binding schemas are standard again.

Rather than discouraging you from using features added by alternate frameworks, this should actually get you excited about the prospect. If you find a framework that adds something you need in an application, you should take advantage of it. Then you can send mail to the JAXB group (*jaxb-feedback@java.sun.com*) and let them know about the features you'd like to see in the Sun framework. Instead of shying away from these features because they aren't in JAXB, I recommend that you do just the opposite; take advantage of them and encourage Sun to embrace them as well.

J2EE

One of the most interesting aspects of data binding is how Sun places it within the J2EE picture. As Sun is prone to do, APIs like JAXB get folded into larger products' APIs; in fact, this is how JAXP made it into the latest version of the Java 2 Enterprise Edition. While this doesn't add any new functionality to the API, it certainly does make it more readily available, especially for those developers using J2EE who may not have yet found a need for data binding. The J2EE implications of data binding are certainly of interest to all enterprise developers.

Data Binding in Enterprise Applications

Some of the most relevant applications for data binding turn out to work with configuration data and messaging. In the first situation, reading XML configuration files becomes trivial with data binding and allows you to avoid writing a lot of SAX or DOM code for a relatively simple purpose. The second situation, messaging, uses data binding to quickly convert between an XML format and Java instance data and back again. Both of these use cases turn out to be prevalent in enterprise applications. In fact, most common uses of data binding end up being prime candidates for enterprise applications. As a result, it's no surprise that J2EE is almost certain to see JAXB added to its laundry list of features.

The interesting aspect of the inclusion of JAXB is that it allows tighter integration between other enterprise components. While it is certainly possible to include additional APIs in your enterprise applications manually, a Sun-handled integration is generally going to encourage developers even further. It also means that applications like servlets, JSPs, EJBs, and the like can all easily reference JAXB-generated classes. Even more importantly, tools like the J2EE SDK reference implementation and vendor application servers like BEA Weblogic and Lutris Enhydra will provide GUIs for running constraints through schema compilers. In other words, using JAXB becomes a piece of cake.

Finally, consider that data binding in J2EE platforms can in turn increase functionality and feature sets supported by the data binding frameworks. With data binding as part of a J2EE platform, it makes sense to move toward data binding for use in the platform internals. For example, reading an *ejb-jar.xml* or *web.xml* deployment descriptor with data binding is a perfectly logical step in adding data binding into a J2EE platform. This results in greater reliance on data binding, which, in turn, results in more stability, more features, and more testing. If this isn't clear, consider that as soon as JAXP 1.0 made it into the J2EE platform, work immediately began on JAXP 1.1 because of missing features important to the J2EE platform internals that relied on JAXP. Expect the same for JAXB; for example, XML Schema support may move up the priority list if the J2EE platform needs to use schemas and wants to rely on data binding for deployment descriptor reading. In other words, JAXB as part of the J2EE specification is, in every sense, a very good thing.

Related APIs

The other important aspect of JAXB's appearance in enterprise applications is that it gains interoperability with related APIs. In the last section, I discussed how inclusion in J2EE would increase its integration with APIs like servlets, JSPs, and EJBs; these orthogonal APIs are generally unrelated to JAXB. However, quite a few of these "JAX" APIs are showing up. In fact, Sun has recently released a "JAX-pack" bundle, which includes the latest release of all of these APIs. Each API serves a different purpose in the Java and XML world. Briefly, I've listed each here in Table 10-1.

Table 10-1. The current JAX-pack

Abbreviation	Name	Purpose
JAXB	Java Architecture for XML Binding	Java-to-XML data binding
JAXM	Java API for XML Messaging	Vendor-neutral approach to SOAP and XML messaging
JAXP	Java API for XML Processing	Vendor-neutral approach to XML parsing and transformations
JAXR	Java API for XML Registries	Java-enabled interaction with ebXML and UDDI registries
JAX-RPC	Java API for XML-based RPC	Vendor-neutral approach to XML-RPC messaging

As you can probably see from the descriptions, all of these APIs are aimed at web services and enterprise applications. Because of this targeting, the APIs will have to interoperate, since many, if not all, could conceivably be used in the same application, in concert. The upshot of all this is that you should expect to see extremely simple connectivity features arise, where (for example) JAXM messages can easily be turned into Java objects via JAXB, UDDI registries can be communicated with via JAXM and JAX-RPC, and JAXP is actually used to determine the parser involved in a JAXB unmarshalling process.

The future for data binding, and in fact all Java and XML APIs, is extremely bright. At this point, you should feel you have a strong grasp on at least the JAXB API and a good start on several open source alternatives. The best thing you can do now is take this conceptual knowledge and apply it practically to some of your own applications, to really get the concepts discussed to sink in. Finally, let us know how you fare; I'm always available via email (see the preface for details on contacting both O'Reilly and me), so I hope to hear from you and see you around online.

Tools Reference

This appendix deals with the tools used by each data binding framework. The schema compiler tools often have numerous command-line switches available to them, and keeping up with them can be a bit of a pain. This appendix should help.

JAXB

Here's a summary of the command-line JAXB class generation tool:

```
C:\dev\jaxb-1.0-ea\lib>java com.sun.tools.xjc.Main
Usage: xjc <schema> [ <binding-schema> ] [ -d <directory> ]
           [ -roots <element-list> ]
```

Table A-1 lists the meaning of each option.

Table A-1. JAXB xjc options

Flag	Value	Purpose
N/A	DTD to parse	Specify the DTD constraint set to JAXB to generate class from.
N/A	Binding schema to parse	Specify the binding schema (if any) to use for generation options.
-d	Destination directory	Specify the directory to put generated classes in.
-roots	List of XML element names	If a DTD has multiple elements that can be considered the root of a document, this option allows listing of each element. JAXB will use this list for generating classes.

Zeus

Here is the output from the Zeus command-line source generation tool:

```
[bmclaugh@aragorn Zeus]$ java org.enhydra.zeus.util.DTDSourceGenerator
Usage: java org.enhydra.zeus.util.DTDSourceGenerator
          -constraints=<constraints filename>
       [-outputDir=<output directory>]
       [-collapseSimpleElements=<true | false>]
       [-ignoreIDAttributes=<true | false>]
       [-javaPackage=<Java package name>]
       [-root=<Root Element Name>]
```

Table A-2 summarizes each option and its purpose.

Table A-2. Zeus DTDSourceGenerator options

Flag	Value	Purpose
-constraints	DTD to parse	Specify the DTD constraint set to Zeus to generate class from.
-javaPackage	Java package	Set package for generated classes.
-outputDir	Destination directory	Specify the directory to put generated classes in.
-collapseSimpleElements	true or false	If true, elements with no attributes are collapsed into their parents and not generated into objects themselves.
-ignoreIDAttributes	true or false	If true, elements with only an ID attribute are also considered simple (see collapseSimpleElements). This is useful when all elements have IDREFs attached to them with no business meaning.
-root	N/A	If a DTD has multiple elements that can be considered the root of a document, this option allows listing of each element. Zeus will use this list for generating classes.

Castor

Here is the output from the Castor generation tool:

```
[bmclaugh@aragorn]$ java org.exolab.castor.builder.SourceGenerator

Usage: -i filename
       [-package package-name]
       [-dest dest-dir]
       [-line-separator ( unix | mac | win)]
       [-f ]
       [-h ]
       [-verbose ]
       [-nodesc ]
       [-types types]
       [-type-factory classname]
       [-nomarshall ]
       [-testable ]
```

Table A-3 details each option and its use.

Table A-3. Castor SourceGenerator options

Flag	Value	Purpose
-i	XML Schema to parse	Specify the schema constraint set to Castor to generate class from.
-package	Java package	Set package for generated classes.
-dest	Destination directory	Set the directory to put generated classes in.
-line-separator	unix or mac or win	Set line separator to use for a specific platform; by default, this will attempt to autodetect your platform.
-f	N/A	Hide nonfatal warnings in class generation.

Table A-3. Castor SourceGenerator options (continued)

Flag	Value	Purpose
-h	N/A	Display a help screen and command usage.
-verbose	N/A	Display extra information about the class generation process.
-nodesc	N/A	Prevent creation of class descriptors.
-types	Type for collections	Specify the collection type to use.
-nomarshall	N/A	Prevent generation of marshal( ) methods on generated classes.
-testable	N/A	Set up class to be used by Castor testing framework (included with Castor).

Quick

Quick provides several utilities that are detailed in the text. Each one is listed here, with the options accepted by that tool.

cfgDtd2Qdml

cfgDtd2Qdml converts from a DTD into a QDML schema. Here is an example of using this tool:

```
[bmclaugh@aragorn]$ sh cfgDtd2Qdml.sh -in=book.dtd -out=book.qdml
```

Table A-4 details each option and its use.

Table A-4. Quick cfgDtd2Qdml options

Flag	Value	Purpose
-in	DTD to parse	Specify the DTD constraint set to Quick to generate QDML from.
-out	QDML file to generate	Specify the filename of the QDML schema to generate.

cfgQdml2Qjml

cfgQdml2Qjml converts from a QDML schema into a QJML binding schema. You will almost always need to make modifications to this generated binding schema to ensure it matches your specific Java classes. Here is an example of usage:

```
[bmclaugh@aragorn xml]$ sh cfgQdml2Qjml.sh -in=book.qdml -out=book.qjml \
    -package=javajaxb.book
```

Table A-5 details each option and its use.

Table A-5. Quick cfgQdml2Qjml options

Flag	Value	Purpose
-in	QDML to parse	Specify the QDML constraint set to Quick to generate QJML from.
-out	QJML file to generate	Specify the filename of the QJML binding schema to generate.
-package	Java package name	The Java package to use as a prefix for all targetClass mappings.

cfgQjml2Java

cfgQjml2Java allows generation of Java source files from a QJML binding schema.

```
C:\dev\javajaxb\ch09\src\xml>cfgQjml2Java -in=book.qjml -out=..\generated
```

Table A-6 details each option and its use.

Table A-6. Quick cfgQjml2Java options

Flag	Value	Purpose
-in	QJML to parse	Specify the QJML binding schema to Quick to generate Java source code from.
-out	Output directory	Specify the directory to generate classes within. Note that if this is not an existing directory, all the output will be merged into a single file with the name specified here.
-printClone	true or false	If true, this will generate an interface and common base class that define the clone() method, which should then be overridden manually in all generated classes. By default, this is set to false.
-printQAware	true or false	If true, this will generate an interface and common base class that make XML-aware methods available. This allows XPath-style navigation through your classes, such as getting the parent or children of a given object. By default, this is set to false.
-printFullConst	true or false	If true, this will generate a constructor for each generated class that takes in all data values for the object. This essentially requires correct formation of the object in Java. If false, only a default, no-args constructor is generated. By default, this is set to true.
-printMoreMethods	true or false	If true, this will print additional utility methods on classes, particularly those with lists of values within them. Unless you are on a device with a very small memory footprint, you should always leave this at the default setting, which is true.
-oneNewClass	true or false	If true, concrete classes are generated. If false, then an abstract class is generated, along with a simple concrete implementation. If you want to make changes to the generated classes, but would prefer to leave the Quick-generated class alone, this can separate what Quick requires (in the base abstract class) and what you do (in your subclass). By default, this is set to true.

A few other options are allowed to the utility. For example, genPackage, setParents, and printPrint are all valid options, and many will change the generated classes. However, several of these options appear to be either buggy or broken at the time of this writing. I expect these problems to be fixed by the time you read this, but as their purpose was unclear, they are left out of this appendix. You can visit Quick online and join the mailing lists to find out more about these specific options.

cfgQdml2Dtd

cfgQdml2Dtd converts from a QDML schema into a DTD. Here is an example of using this tool:

```
[bmclaugh@aragorn xml]$ sh cfgQdml2DTD.sh -in=book.qdml -out=book_from_qdml.dtd
```

Table A-7 details each option and its use.

Table A-7. Quick cfgQdml2Dtd options

Flag	Value	Purpose
-in	QDML to parse	Specify the QDML schema to Quick to generate DTD from.
-out	DTD file to generate	Specify the filename of the DTD to generate.

Quick Source Files

This appendix contains the source files for classes into which the XML documents will be unmarshalled. The examples in Chapter 9 use these classes. Each demonstrates that in addition to data accessor and mutator methods, Quick is capable of converting XML into Java classes that have business methods. All of these classes are also available online at *http://www.newInstance.com.*

Example B-1 is the top of the object tree and represents a purchase order. This can, in turn, store several different orders and also has a business method on it (getTotalPrice()).

Example B-1. The PurchaseOrder class

```
package javajaxb.po;

import java.util.Iterator;
import java.util.LinkedList;
import java.util.List;

public class PurchaseOrder {

    /** The list of <code>{@link Order}</code> objects */
    protected List orderList;

    public PurchaseOrder() {
        this(new LinkedList());
    }

    public PurchaseOrder(List orderList) {
        if (orderList != null) {
            this.orderList = orderList;
        } else {
            this.orderList = new LinkedList();
        }
    }

    public List getOrderList() {
```

```
        return orderList;
    }

    public void setOrderList(List orderList) {
        this.orderList = orderList;
    }

    public void addOrder(Order order) {
        orderList.add(order);
    }

    public float getTotalPrice( ) {
        if (orderList == null) {
            return 0;
        }

        float totalPrice = 0;
        for (Iterator i = orderList.iterator(); i.hasNext( ); ) {
            Order order = (Order)i.next( );
            totalPrice += order.getStock().getQuantity() * order.getPurchasePrice( );
        }
        return totalPrice;
    }
}
```

Example B-2 represents the orders stored by this PO.

Example B-2. The order class

```
package javajaxb.po;

public class Order {

    /** The ID of this order */
    private int id;

    /** The SKU of this order */
    private String sku;

    /** The name of the product ordered */
    private String productName;

    /** The manufacturer of the product ordered */
    private String manufacturerName;

    /** The price ordered at */
    private float purchasePrice;

    /** The <code>{@link Stock}</code> item for this order */
    private Stock stock;

    public Order( ) { }
```

Example B-2. The order class (continued)

```java
    public Order(int id, String sku) {
        this.id = id;
        this.sku = sku;
    }

    public int getId( ) {
        return id;
    }

    public void setId(int id) {
        this.id = id;
    }

    public String getSku( ) {
        return sku;
    }

    public void setSku(String sku) {
        this.sku = sku;
    }

    public String getProductName( ) {
        return productName;
    }

    public void setProductName(String productName) {
        this.productName = productName;
    }

    public String getManufacturerName( ) {
        return manufacturerName;
    }

    public void setManufacturerName(String manufacturerName) {
        this.manufacturerName = manufacturerName;
    }

    public float getPurchasePrice( ) {
        return purchasePrice;
    }

    public void setPurchasePrice(float purchasePrice) {
        this.purchasePrice = purchasePrice;
    }

    public Stock getStock( ) {
        return stock;
    }

    public void setStock(Stock stock) {
        this.stock = stock;
    }
}
```

Example B-3 is the stock class, used to indicate quantities and whether to store inventory on hand.

Example B-3. The stock class

```java
package javajaxb.po;

public class Stock {

    /** Whether the stock should be kept on hand */
    private boolean onHand;

    /** The number to order */
    private int quantity;

    public Stock( ) { }

    public Stock(int quantity) {
        this(quantity, true);
    }

    public Stock(int quantity, boolean onHand) {
        this.quantity = quantity;
        this.onHand = onHand;
    }

    public boolean getOnHand( ) {
        return onHand;
    }

    public void setOnHand(boolean onHand) {
        this.onHand = onHand;
    }

    public int getQuantity( ) {
        return quantity;
    }

    public void setQuantity(int quantity) {
        this.quantity = quantity;
    }
}
```

Index

We'd like to hear your suggestions for improving our indexes. Send email to *index@oreilly.com*.

source files, 188
unmarshalling, 163
  converting DTDs to QDML, 164–166
  converting QDML to QJML, 166
  final conversion, 168
  Java classes and, 163
  process, 168–172
web site, 11, 162

R

Relax constraint model, 23
Relax NG, 23
  Zeus and, 123
RelaxBinder (Zeus), 117
remote element, Zeus, 122
resolveEntity( ) method, 16
rest element, 105
result objects, unmarshalling and, 49
resultant XML, marshalling, 73
root attribute, 39
  element element, 100
root element, Zeus, 126

S

SAX API, 3, 13
  class generation, 16
  data binding and, 6
  entity resolution, 14
  hierarchical data and, 16
  methods, 13
  objects, 13
  org.xml.sax.EntityResolver interface, 15
  parsers, XMLScanner instance and, 59
  Zeus and, 131
semantic equivalents, 90
sequence element, 104
server, marshalling, XML conversion and, 81
simple elements
  constraints, 35
  Zeus, 122
SOAP (Simple Object Access Protocol), 7, 17
  data binding and, 19
source code, 31
  compiling, javac, 31
  downloading examples, 34
  Quick, 188
source files (Java), generating, 38–46
sourceGen script (Castor), 138
SourceGenerator class (Castor), 135
  options, 140, 184

static methods, 49
streaming
  APIs and, 3
  output, marshalling and, 84
  unmarshalling results and, 57
string type, DTD constraint model, 23
strings, converting to object instances, 109
Sun EJB DTD, EntityResolver and, 15
supertype attribute, 114

T

transformers, Zeus, 117
trees
  DOM, 4
  SAX API, 3
Trex constraint model, 23
type attribute (element element), 99
type safety, 115
type safety, DTDs, 23
-types option (SourceGenerator class), 141
typing savings, DTD naming conventions
  and, 20

U

UDDI registries, 19
unmarshal( ) method, 47, 48
  Dispatcher instance, 60
unmarshallable attribute, 98
Unmarshaller class (JAXB), 59
unmarshalling, 8
  binding schemas, global options, 98
  Castor, 142–144
    process flow, 136
  intermediate objects and, 59
  Java conversion, 48
  process flow, 47
  Quick, 163
    converting DTDs to QDML, 164–166
    converting QDML to QJML, 166
    final conversion, 168
    Java classes and, 163
    process, 168–172
  resolveEntity( ) method and, 16
  result objects, 49
  results, streaming and, 57
  XML data, 48
  XML data to Java, 50–56
  XML input, 56
  Zeus, 118, 123–128
utilities, Arguments utility class, 85

About the Author

Brett McLaughlin has been working in computers since the Logo days. (Remember the little triangle?) Over the last eight years, Brett has built large-scale enterprise applications for Nextel Communications, Allegiance Telecom, and Lutris Technologies. He has been instrumental in the open source community, contributing to the JDOM and Zeus projects and cofounding the Turbine project. He is also a committer on numerous open source projects, such as JBoss and Apache Cocoon. In an effort to devote more time to teaching others about these technologies, Brett now writes and edits full-time for O'Reilly & Associates. He always has at least one new book in the works and can be found on the open source mailing lists day and night.

Colophon

Our look is the result of reader comments, our own experimentation, and feedback from distribution channels. Distinctive covers complement our distinctive approach to technical topics, breathing personality and life into potentially dry subjects.

The animal on the cover of *Java and XML Data Binding* is an osprey. The osprey is found near lakes, rivers, and seacoasts in every continent except Antarctica. It is especially common in Finland, Scandinavia, and the Chesapeake Bay in the United States. Ospreys are birds of prey with a large wingspan and sharp talons. Most are identified by a small, narrow head, a brown back, and a white stomach. The bird, which eats only fish, feeds two times a day, at mid-morning and in the late afternoon. It hovers over the water, swoops down, and grabs it prey. Then it rests briefly on the water before it flies off to eat its meal.

Ospreys build their nests close to bodies of water. The birds seek sites near food that are surrounded by open space so they can move their large wings easily. Ospreys often choose nesting sites in tall, single trees, power poles, and radio and light towers.

The osprey was nearly an endangered species for many years. Fishing communities sometimes hunted the bird because they feared it would consume valuable fish resources. Industrialization, deforestation, and global population growth were other major threats to the osprey. The use of DDT after World War II also killed a large portion of the osprey population, since this chemical, used to kill insects, also poisoned fish and birds. The pesticide was eventually banned in the United States, but is still a danger to osprey populations in other areas of the world.

Conservation efforts and legal measures have reversed the osprey's shrinking numbers, and the bird is now returning to some of its old habitats. Efforts to build nests for the osprey and reintroduce it to water sources where it once lived have been very successful. Hunting by sports enthusiasts and fishing communities is also a lesser threat to the bird; the 1973 passage of the Endangered Species Act criminalized osprey hunting.

Ann Schirmer was the production editor and proofreader, and Norma Emory was the copyeditor, for *Java and XML Data Binding*. Claire Cloutier, Tatiana Apandi Diaz, and Sarah Sherman provided quality control. Tom Dinse wrote the index.

Hanna Dyer designed the cover of this book, based on a series design by Edie Freedman. The cover image is a 19th-century engraving from the Dover Pictorial Archive. Emma Colby produced the cover layout with QuarkXPress 4.1 using Adobe's ITC Garamond font.

Melanie Wang designed the interior layout, based on a series design by David Futato. This book was converted to FrameMaker 5.5.6 with a format conversion tool created by Erik Ray, Jason McIntosh, Neil Walls, and Mike Sierra that uses Perl and XML technologies. The text font is Linotype Birka; the heading font is Adobe Myriad Condensed; and the code font is LucasFont's TheSans Mono Condensed. The illustrations that appear in the book were produced by Robert Romano and Jessamyn Read using Macromedia FreeHand 9 and Adobe Photoshop 6. The tip and warning icons were drawn by Christopher Bing. This colophon was written by Ann Schirmer.

 # More Titles from O'Reilly

Java In a Nutshell Quick References

Java Enterprise in a Nutshell, 2nd Edition

By David Flanagan, Jim Farley &
William Crawford
2nd Edition April 2002
992 pages, ISBN 0-596-00152-5

Completely revised and updated to cover the
new 2.0 version of Sun Microsystems Java
Enterprise Edition software, *Java Enterprise
in a Nutshell* 2nd edition covers the RMI,
Java IDL, JDBC, JNDI, Java Servlet, and Enterprise JavaBeans APIs, with a fast-paced tutorial and compact reference material on each technology.

Java Foundation Classes in a Nutshell

By David Flanagan
1st Edition September 1999
748 pages, ISBN 1-56592-488-6

Java Foundation Classes in a Nutshell
provides an in-depth overview of the important
pieces of the (JFC), such as the Swing components and Java 2D. It also includes compact
reference material on all the GUI- and graphics-
related classes in the numerous javax.swing
and java.awt packages. Covers Java 2.

J2ME in a Nutshell

By Kim Topley
1st Edition, March 2002
462 pages, ISBN 0-596-00253-X

O'Reilly's *J2ME in a Nutshell* is as definitive a
reference to the heart of the J2ME platform
as the classic *Java in a Nutshell* is for the
Standard Java platform. Its solid introduction
to J2ME covers the essential APIs for different
types of devices and deployments; the profiles
(specifications of the minimum sets of APIs
useful for a set-top box, wireless phone, PDA, or other device);
and the Java virtual machine functions that support those APIs.
The meat of the book is its classic O'Reilly-style quick reference
to all the core Micro Edition classes.

Java in a Nutshell, 4th Edition

By David Flanagan
4th Edition March 2002
992 pages, ISBN 0-596-00283-1

This bestselling quick reference contains an
accelerated introduction to the Java programming language and its key APIs, so seasoned
programmers can start writing Java code right
away. The fourth edition of *Java in a Nutshell*
covers the new Java 1.4 beta edition, which contains significant changes from the 1.3 version.

Java Examples in a Nutshell, 2nd Edition

By David Flanagan
2nd Edition September 2000
584 pages, ISBN 0-596-00039-1

In *Java Examples in a Nutshell*, the author
of Java in a Nutshell has created an entire
book of example programs that not only
serve as great learning tools, but can also be
modified for individual use. The second edition of this best-selling book covers Java 1.3,
and includes new chapters on JSP and
servlets, XML, Swing, and Java 2D. This is the book for those who
learn best "by example."

O'REILLY®

How to stay in touch with O'Reilly

1. Visit our award-winning web site

http://www.oreilly.com/

★ "Top 100 Sites on the Web"—PC Magazine
★ CIO Magazine's Web Business 50 Awards

Our web site contains a library of comprehensive product information (including book excerpts and tables of contents), downloadable software, background articles, interviews with technology leaders, links to relevant sites, book cover art, and more. File us in your bookmarks or favorites!

2. Join our email mailing lists

Sign up to get email announcements of new books and conferences, special offers, and O'Reilly Network technology newsletters at:

http://www.elists.oreilly.com

It's easy to customize your free elists subscription so you'll get exactly the O'Reilly news you want.

3. Get examples from our books

To find example files for a book, go to:

http://www.oreilly.com/catalog

select the book, and follow the "Examples" link.

4. Work with us

Check out our web site for current employment opportunites:

http://jobs.oreilly.com/

5. Register your book

Register your book at:

http://register.oreilly.com

6. Contact us

O'Reilly & Associates, Inc.
1005 Gravenstein Hwy North
Sebastopol, CA 95472 USA
TEL: 707-827-7000 or 800-998-9938
            (6am to 5pm PST)
FAX: 707-829-0104

order@oreilly.com
For answers to problems regarding your order or our products. To place a book order online visit:

http://www.oreilly.com/order_new/

catalog@oreilly.com
To request a copy of our latest catalog.

booktech@oreilly.com
For book content technical questions or corrections.

proposals@oreilly.com
To submit new book proposals to our editors and product managers.

international@oreilly.com
For information about our international distributors or translation queries. For a list of our distributors outside of North America check out:

http://international.oreilly.com/distributors.html

O'REILLY®